THE ARC OF THE STORM

Elisavietta Ritchie

SIGNAL BOOKS
Chapel Hill, NC

For Chris Brookhouse —
Even if you did not have
a direct hand in this
book, I thank you for
your help in keeping
Signal Books alive.
Dougald edited the
manuscript, and he
was always on target.

Elisavietta Ritchie

Other books by the author:

ELEGY FOR THE OTHER WOMAN:
   NEW AND SELECTED TERRIBLY FEMALE POEMS (1996)

WILD GARLIC: THE JOURNAL OF MARIA X
   (novella in verse, 1995)

A WOUND-UP CAT AND OTHER BEDTIME STORIES
   (poetry, 1993)

FLYING TIME: STORIES AND HALF-STORIES
   (fiction, 1992 & 1996)

THE PROBLEM WITH EDEN (poetry, 1985)

RAKING THE SNOW (poetry, 1982)

MOVING TO LARGER QUARTERS (poetry, 1977)

A SHEATH OF DREAMS AND OTHER GAMES (poetry, 1976)

TIGHTENING THE CIRCLE OVER EEL COUNTRY
   (poetry, 1974)

TIMBOT (novella in verse, 1970)

Poetry anthologies edited:

THE DOLPHIN'S ARC: POEMS ON ENDANGERED
   CREATURES OF THE SEA

FINDING THE NAME

Translations:

THE TWELVE, by Aleksandr Blok

THE ARC OF THE STORM

Library of Congress Cataloging-in-Publication Data

Ritchie, Elisavietta
    The arc of the storm
        p.   cm.
    ISBN 0-930095-06-5
    PS3568.I8A89   1998   96-34926
    811'.54--DC20   CIP

For book orders:
SIGNAL BOOKS   Elisavietta A Ritchie
7117 Tyndall Court   PO Box 298
Raleigh, NC 27615   Broomes Island MD 20615-0298
e-mail: gtkach@worldnet.att.net
phone & fax: (919) 870-8505

Book design by Michael Brown
Cover production by Cassio Lynm
Author's photograph by Clyde Henri Farnsworth
Production by Andrew Smyth and Roxanne Henderson

Printed in the United States of America

ACKNOWLEDGMENTS

The author thanks the editors of publications in which many of these poems appeared, often in earlier versions:

"After The Last Note of a Harp Recital": *Harp Strings*, 1995.

"Afterthought": *New York Quarterly; Out of A/Maze: On The Mentally Distinct*, Rochelle Holt, editor, Rose Shell Press, 1996. Also incorporated into story "Sounds," a PEN Syndicated Fiction winner broadcast over National Public Radio, and published in *Passager*, and *Flying Time: Stories and Half-Stories*, Signal Books, © 1992 & 1996, Elisavietta Ritchie; *Generation to Generation*, Sandra Martz and Shirley Coe, editors, Papier-Maché Press, 1998.

"Aide-Memoire": *The Flutes of Power*, Great Elm Press, 1995; *New to North America: Writing by Immigrants, Their Children & Grandchildren*, Abby Bogomolny, editor, Burning Bush Publications, 1998; *The Great Blue Heron and Other Poems*, Adrienne Lee Press, 1998; as "Note to a Poet in Exile": *PEN's Writers-in-Exile*, 1988.

"Annunciations, September": *Visions*, 1989; *Free State*, Stacy Tuthill, editor, SCOP Publications Inc., 1990; *Women of the Fourteenth Moon*, Amber Sumrall, editor, The Crossing Press, 1991; *Each in Her Own Way*, Elizabeth Claman, editor, Queen of Swords Press, 1994.

"In the Archives": Reprinted by permission of the Poetry Society of America. Originally published in *The Poetry Review*, Vol. 2, No. 1, Fall, 1984, © 1984, Elisavietta Ritchie; *Finding The Name*, The Wineberry Press, 1983.

"As The Old Spy Picks Up A First-Century B.C. Perfume Bottle...": *Exquisite Corpse*, 1988; *The Problem With Eden*, Armstrong State College Press, © 1985, Elisavietta Ritchie; *A Wound-Up Cat and Other Bedtime Stories*, Palmerston Press, © 1993, Elisavietta Ritchie; *Hold The Macho*, in press.

"Bedtime Stories": *The American Scholar*, Vol. 61, No.1, Winter, 1992; © 1992 by the author; *A Wound-Up Cat and Other Bedtime Stories*.

"Beyond The Asparagus Field": *Poet's Domain*, 1990; *Georgia Poetry Society Yearbook*.

"Beyond Little Black River, Manitoba": *The Christian Science Monitor*, © 1995.

"Bossa Nova": *Spectrum*, 1984; *Yellow Umbrella; Annual Anthology of American Verse*, 1985.

"Breaking Formation": *If I Had A Hammer: Women's Work*, Sandra Martz, editor, Papier-Maché Press, 1990; reprinted in prose form as part of story "Sounds", a PEN Syndicated Fiction winner broadcast over National Public Radio; *Flying Time: Stories and Half-Stories; Generation to Generation*; to be in anthology of women with chronic illness, Laurel Fain, editor.

"Cacophonies": *New York Quarterly*, 1995; *Hungry As We Are: XXth anniversary anthology of Washington area poets*, Ann Darr, editor, Washington Writers Publishing House, 1995.

"Companions": *Earth's Daughters, Doppelganger* issue, 1995; *Staring Back: Writers With Disabilities*, Kenny Fries, editor, Dutton, 1998.

"Correspondence With A Russian Sailor": *Cincinnati Poetry Review, 1988*.

"Covert Matters, Sofia": *Poetry Now, 1980; Gnosis*, 1984.

"Creative Acts": *Canadian Writers' Journal*, 1995.

"Discovery: Perhentian Island, Malaysia": *Rye Bread: Women Poets Rising*, Stacy Tuthill, editor, SCOP Publications Inc., 1977.

"Door Steps": *Portals*, in press.

"A Dream of Siberia in April": *Gypsy*, winner, 1989 Amnesty International Award; *A Wound-Up Cat and Other Bedtime Stories*.

"Early Versions": *Descant*, Winter, 1997.

"En Route To A Bone Scan": *Arc*, # 31, Autumn 1993; *Hot Flashes: Women on the Change of Life*, Lynne Taetzsch, editor, Faber & Faber, 1995; and in *Staring Back: Writers With Disabilities*.

"In The Early Days of the War": *Kalliope: a journal of women's art*, Secrets Issue, including audio version, 1997.

"On The Eve of a Salvation Army Pickup": *Caprice*, 1996.

"Expatriates": verse version in *Unicorns and Space Stations*, 1995; prose version in *Helmsman*, 1995.

"Family Matters": *Atlanta Review*, 1996.

"Flutter Kicking Through Foreign Waves": *Descant*, Winter, 1996.

"Flying Time": *Home Planet News*; included in story "Flying Time", a winner in the 1986 PEN Syndicated Fiction and *Amelia*, Reed Smith competitions; *Flying Time: Stories and Half-Stories; A Wound-Up Cat and Other Bedtime Stories; Grow Old Along With Me — The Best Is Yet To Be*, Sandra Martz, editor, Papier-Maché Press, 1996.

"Four Potatoes": *Canadian Women's Studies*, Vol. 16, No. 3, 1996.

"From The Collected Works": *The Christian Science Monitor* © 1993.

"Geometry on the Toronto Ferry": *The Christian Science Monitor* © 1992.

"Ghosts": as "Family Ghosts" in *Cincinnati Poetry Review*, 1995.

"Giant Cameroonian Frog": *Stone Country*, 1988; *Ribet: A Celebration of Frogs and Toads*, Jill Carpenter, editor, 1998.

"Great Aunt Eleanora Defends Her Decision to Remain on Her Farm, Although At Night, Of Course There Are Sounds": *Passager*, 1990; poem also incorporated into story "Sounds", a PEN Syndicated Fiction winner, reprinted in *Flying Time: Stories and Half-Stories; Generation to Generation*.

"Hand-To-Mouth": *Amelia* (winner 1994 Marguerette Cummins Quarterly Broadside Award); *Who Cares*, in press.

"Harvestimes": *Poet Lore*.

"Hibiscus Child": *Kairos*, 1994.

"Icarus, Manhattan": *New York Quarterly*, 1997; *The XY Files: The Truth About Men*, Nancy Fry, editor, Sherman Asher Publishing, 1997.

"In His Tiger Cage, The Prisoner of War": *Amelia; Freedom's Just Another*

Word...Whitney Scott, editor, Outrider Press, 1998.

"In The Balkan Hotel": as "Unfinished Journal" in *The Poetry Review*. Reprinted by permission of the Poetry Society of America. Originally published in *The Poetry Review* Vol. 2, No. 1, Fall, l984. Copyright 1984 by the author.

"In This Winged Instant": *The Christian Science Monitor*, © 1995; *Potomac Review*, 1996.

"In Your Absence": *Descant*, Winter, 1997.

"I've Never Written a Baseball Poem": *The Christian Science Monitor*, © 1985; *Fan*, 1993; *Diamonds Are A Girl's Best Friend*, Elinor Nauen, editor, Faber & Faber, 1994.

"Korean Landscape, 1977": *The Hermit Kingdom*, Paul Edwards, editor, 1995; as "Another War, Another April: Korea 1977" translated into Korean in *Moonhak Sasong*, 1977.

"Lessons, Nantucket Harbor": *Poets On; Helmsman*, 1995; also transformed in story "Re-inventing The Archives," *Gifts Of Our Fathers*, Thomas Verny, editor, Crossing Press, 1994.

"Letter from Belgrade": *The Christian Science Monitor*, © 1979.

"Like My Aunts": *Canadian Women's Studies*, 1994.

"Lilacs": *Embrys Journal*, 1995; *Family: The Possibility of Tradition*, editor, Jim Villani, Pig Iron Press, in press.

"Mail Order: 'The Ultimate Sportsman's Knife'": *Canadian Women's Studies*, 1993.

"Marine Life": as "Phenomena" in *Earth Tones*, Belinda Subraham, editor, Vergin Press, 1993; *Poets For A Liveable Planet*, 1994.

"May Day Moon": *Ann Arbor Review*, 1977; *The Stable Companion*, 1995; translated into Malay and Indonesian for *Berita Buana*, 1978; *Budaya Jaya*, 1978.

"The Memory Requirement": *Poets On: Forgetting*, 1994.

"Mid-October Report From The Roof Of The World": *Negative Capability*, (finalist in 1995 St. Agnes Eve Contest), 1998.

"Mudang: The Shamans of Korea": *Canadian Women's Studies*, Vol. 16, No. 3, 1996.

"Mushroom Merchant, Korea": *Ann Arbor Review*, 1978.

"My Daughter Borrows Two Eggs": *New York Quarterly*, 1989; Library of Congress flyer; *Family: The Possibility of Tradition*.

"North of the Air Base, At Home": *Swamp Root*, Vol. 6, 1990.

"Nothing, One Evening, Kyoto": *Home Planet News*, 1978.

"Not Just About A Squirrel, Of Course": *The Ledge*, (First Prize, 1995 Annual Poetry Contest), 1996.

"The Odd One: On Seeing A Photo of Teilhard de Chardin *en famille*": *Press*, Vol. 1, No. 1, 1996.

"The Old Bridge, After The War": *Silver Quill* (Second Prize, 1995 David Ross Memorial Poetry competition), 1996.

"On Opening A Brand-New Half-Stitched Book of Poetry": *The Christian Science Monitor*, © 1985.

"Pastoral Letter": *New York Quarterly*, 1993.

"The Peaceable Kingdom": *Architrave, A Journal of the Arts,* 1996; *A Practice of Peace,* Judith Asher, editor, Sherman Asher Publishing, 1998.

"The Persistence of Bears": *Poetpourri,* 1996.

"Place Settings": *Mothers and Daughters,* June Cottner, editor, 1998.

"A Poet's Flat, Moscow": *Cincinnati Poetry Review,* 1987.

"Postcard From The Arctic": *Amelia,* (1993 "Amelia" Prize); *Kairos,* 1993; transformed in story "Re-inventing The Archives", *Gifts Of Our Fathers.*

"Power Outage": *eleven,* 1984.

"Provolone": *Metropolitain,* 1992.

"Radishes?": *Radishes and Flowers; Metropolitain,* 1992; prose version, *The Christian Science Monitor,* © 1996.

"Reading The Stones": *Quantum Tao,* Blue Heron Press, 1996.

"On The Red Arrow Express": *The Christian Science Monitor,* © 1992; *A Wound-Up Cat and Other Bedtime Stories; Exit 13,* 1995; also recycled into story "Teatime In Leningrad," *Flying Time: Stories and Half-Stories; Two Worlds Walking,* C.W. Truesdale and Diane Glancy, editors, New Rivers Press, 1995.

"Red Dreams": *Poetpourri* (finalist in 1995 competition), 1996.

"Report From The District: Toxic Problems": as "Urban Report: Disposal Problems": *The Poet's Domain,* 1990; *The Singing Bridge; WPFW Poetry Anthology,* Grace Cavalieri, editor, 1992; *A Wound-Up Cat & Other Bedtime Stories.*

"On a Request To Gather Puffballs": *Metropolitain,* 1992; *Maryland Poetry Review,* 1992.

"Residents": *The Christian Science Monitor,* © 1992.

"Sand Hill": *Potomac Review,* 1997.

"Sarajevo": part one, *The Christian Science Monitor,* © 1990; part two, *Home Planet News,* 1990; *Raking The Snow,* Washington Writers' Publishing House, © 1982, Elisavietta Ritchie.

"Saucers": *Home Planet News,* 1997.

"Scooping The Moon": *The Christian Science Monitor,* © 1996; earlier version published as "Three Reality Haiku" in *Lotus Leaves,* 1995.

"Sentries" (published as two poems, "Sentries" and "Impasse"): *Christian Science Monitor,* © 1996.

"Seer, Surabaya": *Freedom's Just Another Word...*Whitney Scott, editor, Outrider Press, 1998.

"Silver": as "From Goodwill," *The Christian Science Monitor,* © 1994.

"Sisterhood": *Women: A Journal of Liberation; A Sheath Of Dreams And Other Games,* Proteus Press, © 1976, Elisavietta Ritchie; transformed in story "Re-inventing The Archives" for *Gifts Of Our Fathers.*

"Skipping Games": *Canadian Women's Studies,* 1995.

"Sorting Laundry": © *Poetry* 1988, Modern Poetry Society; *Sound and Sense,* 8th Edition, Perrine and Arp, editors, Harcourt Brace Jovanovich Inc. 1991; *Flying Time: Stories & Half-Stories;*

A Wound-Up Cat and Other Bedtime Stories.
"Staying Awake on Mount San Angelo": *Potomac Review,* 1995.
"Stoned Fruit": *Caprice,* 1996.
"Stranger Moons": *The Christian Science Monitor,* © 1994.
"Swan Lake": *The American Scholar,* Vol. 66, No.4, Autumn, 1997 © 1997
    Phi Beta Kappa Society.
"Tabula Rasa": *New York Quarterly,* 1996.
"Terra Irredenta: The Elder Speaks": *Passager,* 1996.
"Them": *Outsiders / Sunk Island Review,* 1995; *Amelia* (1994 Encore
    Award).
"Toad, Sungai Karang, Malaysia": *Ribet: A Celebration of Frogs and Toads.*
"To Ride The White Camel": *Poet Lore,* 1985.
"The Transport of Klaus von Z.": *Amelia,* in press; *Outsiders / Sunk Island
    Review,* 1995.
"Unscheduled Flights": *C.R.E.A.T.E.: Journal of the Creative and Expressive
    Arts Therapies Exchange,* May, 1995; *Dream Network Journal,* 1995.
"Visitations, Park Avenue": as "Visitations: Manhattan": *Pulpsmith,* 1984.
"Visitations, the Virginia Center for the Creative Arts": prose version,
    The Christian Science Monitor, © 1994.
"Visiting Great Aunt Eugenya by the Chesapeake": *The American Scholar,*
    Vol. 65, No. 4, Autumn 1996, © 1996 The Phi Beta Kappa Society.
"Visiting Hours": *Blue Unicorn,* 1983; *JAMA: Journal of the American
    Medical Association,* 1990.
"Watching TV From The Check-Out Counter At The Five-&-Dime":
    Metropolitain, 1992.
"Why Some Nights I Go To Bed Without Undressing": *Full Moon,* 1984;
    Empty Window Review, 1985; *Out of Season,* Paula Trachtman,
    editor, Amagansett Press, 1993; *Ladies, Start Your Engines,* Elinor
    Nauen, editor, Faber & Faber, 1997; *A Stranger at My Table: Women
    Writing About Mothering Adolescents,* Helen Braid, editor, The
    Women's Press Ltd., London, 1997.
"Witness": *The Ledge,* No. 21, Spring 1997; *Details Omitted From The Text,*
    Shulamit Wechter Caine and Karen Alkalay-Gut, editors, in press.

The author wishes to express her gratitude for encouragement and practical help from:

The PEN Syndicated Fiction Project for four awards;
The DC Commission for the Arts and Humanities for four Individual Artist Grants;
The Virginia Center for the Creative Arts for several fellowships;
Colleen Perrin of The Palmerston Press, Toronto;
The Washington Writers Publishing House;

And for their editorial assistance and encouragement:

Clyde Henri Farnsworth, Shirley Cochrane, Suzanne Collins, Maxine Combs, Mary Edsall, Elizabeth Follin-Jones, David Henderson, Faith Jackson, Vivette Kady, Mary Sue Koeppel, Ann Knox, Merrill Leffler, Jim Nason, Elisabeth Stevens, Richard Rosenman, Elisabeth Stevens, Barbara Williams, and especially Dougald McMillan of Signal Books of Chapel Hill.

for Clyde Henri Farnsworth

CONTENTS

VIII. THRIFT AND GOODWILL

IX. IN THIS WINGED INSTANT

I.
FAMILY AFFAIRS

LESSONS, NANTUCKET HARBOR

Surrounded by flounder,
salt in our hair,
my father and I kneel on a pier.

We're sunburned after all day
in a small open boat.
I am six, my father — ?

He doesn't seem old.
He is handsome, charming,
his moustache is trim.

◆ ◆ ◆

How many women has he
already loved…I grow up
to love many men.

Does he ever wonder about
this part of my life…He tells me
of his affairs one afternoon

while records spin gypsy guitars
and in the next room, without warning
my mother dumbfounds us by dying.

◆ ◆ ◆

At six, I worry only how will we clean
all these platter-shaped fish
whose eyes migrated topside.

My father takes a thin knife,
slits bellies, dumps guts
for minnows darting like bees.

Then he teaches me to filet:
grip the throat of the tail,
slice terribly close to the bones.

1

SKIPPING GAMES

"Skip rope," he says,
"it's good for hearts."

And I am six
and can't keep up
with rhyming games
the bigger girls
with double ropes
jump over, through,
like circus dogs
or seals through hoops.

I'd rather climb
the trees with boys.

Whatever sport,
I still end up
with knotted lines,
entangled limbs,
a jumbled heart
ensnared in skeins
it will require
my entire life
to ravel out.

IN THE EARLY DAYS OF THE WAR

My father beams at me from England.
Behind him, trees, and a tower, squared.
The top, I imagine, must be bombed:
in Philadelphia our church is spired.

He will soon move on to the front.
His well-pressed uniform will get
dusty, bloody, torn. Aged eight,
an ocean away, I read headlines.

At nineteen I visit an exquisite
English lady among her beds
of rosemary, savory, lavender
drawing ten species of bees.

On her bureau stands the duplicate
of the black-and-white photo on mine.
"I used my last film on him," she sighs.
Her husband off in India, Malaya, Burma,

she billeted officers in her house, she had
plenty of space. "And," he later tells me
but not my mother, "sympathy." He smiles.
I did not know to judge then, won't now.

SISTERHOOD

My half-sister may still survive
beneath the palms of Marrakesh.

Our father told me later
of his lovely Moorish housekeeper
one hiatus early in the war.

Although she surely found
new employers and new loves
when Daddy traveled on,
she kept to term his legacy
cherished or embarrassing.

When he came home at last,
looked at me, he surely wondered
if that other daughter too inherited
his freckles, blue eyes, carrot hair?

Or did her mother's duskiness predominate?

Years pass. Oceans apart, we've both
grown up, unknown to one another…

Did she in turn bear throw-back babies,
maintain his distant dynasty,

or abandon them beyond the city gates
before they breathed the desert air
and shocked the tribe with unexpected
freckles, carrot hair, blue eyes?

My sister, are you leading revolutions
or a herd of donkeys to the waterhole?

SWAN LAKE

Never have I flung
even a rag in anger
or smashed a glass to celebrate.

But again I've left my mother
sprawled on her couch,
gin not quite cached.

When like a bride
I begged my husband,
"Help me help her somehow —"

he shrugged,
finished the scotch,
went to bed.

This is not one of those
currently fashionable tales
of wife beating or child abuse:

We still love each other,
our children sleep upstairs,
adored, unbruised.

But tonight in the small house
painted hunter's green,
ringed with hemlocks

in a cul-de-sac, I spin out
my precious set of 78s,
twirling my own choreographies

around and around and around
as I did on childhood afternoons
in my parents' empty apartment,

two-faced Odile/Odette
awkward, out of step,
every dance in the dark,

alone with two brilliant alcoholics
and two children who might have
inherited our proclivities, genes.

I still adore Tchaikovsky
with what my husband calls
"that sloppy passion of adolescence,"

but I gain no wisdom from watching
the needle circling in spirals,
following mysterious molded grooves

never quite coming back to themselves.
When the last 78 spins to a stop,
one by one I let them fall.

Nothing dramatic.
Just quiet crashes
shattering utterly.

SAUCERS

All that is left
of my mother's set
of white pottery rimmed
with sky-blue
are the saucers.

I use them under
clay pots of chives,
oregano, dill, impatiens.

She smashed all
the plates and cups
(alcoholic nights,
mornings shaky).

Summers, plants go
back in the garden,
leaving the saucers
muddy, stained, unfit
even to store.

But I remember
my mother, and scrub
every saucer, soak
hours in bleach,
then slide them
under iced tea.

In autumn they're back
under the pots again,
year after year
till they also break.

Now, like old black women
in South Carolina
who place broken plates
on family graves,
I arrange blue-and-white
saucer shards
around the perimeter
of my yard.

POSTCARD FROM THE ARCTIC

For Roy Tester

1.

Put out for adoption at birth, now
you send me a trio of polar bears:
the mother, dark muzzled, leads
two cubs over the floes. Her feet
stand square on one raft of ice.

The camera caught the first cub
in his mother's wake, front paws
on her float, his black nose
close behind her white tail,
like Babar's procession of elephants.

His back feet stretch from the floe
slipping away behind and he is about
to belly flop into the drink —
His twin stares toward the lens as if,
when he's grown, he would eat it.

Floes shift like lily pads in a summer pond.
Drifting islets of ice extend
toward polar infinity, will freeze
into solid crust when the Wise Crone
snatches away the sun in a cat's-cradle.

2.

Ignorant of your parents,
no offspring of your own
(one learns to be careful),
did you choose this card
half-aware of an inner longing?

Or did you sense that like Mother Bear,
I still try to guide my progeny
through dangerous passages —
even in our more temperate zone,
the world can be slippery. Cold.

3.

I picture you trudging across urban snow
into a brick municipal hall. You seek
a sign: ORIGINS INFORMATION CENTRE.
Day after day, you wait in line,
snowy boots puddle into dark seas,

questions leave more question marks.
Like navigating through Arctic straits:
icebergs surround you, blizzards engulf
your charts scratched on ice, what you
hoped was safe harbor is icebound.

4.

Children irked with imperfect parents
imagine: *I was adopted, my real dad
is the Storm King, my mother — the Snow Queen.*
Yet we are all scions of princes
raised by the shepherd's wife.

Locked in the vault, our crowns await us.
Minions will rush with welcoming roses.
Our kingdoms stretch rich and green.
Meanwhile, we tend royal sheep
whiter, more woolly, than polar bears.

SAND HILL

for Elizabeth Anne Ritchie

"If you get on top of the hill
you'll never die," says the child
patting sand, damp from a week of rain.
"You have to be able to touch the peak."

Around it she builds a wall too high
for wingless insects to cross,
they keep tumbling back in her moat.
She crowns the crest with a feather.

The sun, hidden by fog curling over the shore,
enfolding wavering figures in scrim,
still pours onto our heads.
Observing death waft in quietly,

harming no one yet, I know: in climbing
this particular alp I'd only smash
the mound to infinite grains of sand,
myself to finite splinters of bone.

When we leave the beach
all that's left are footprints,
finger trails, traces of moat,
rays of recalcitrant light.

THE ODD ONE

On seeing a photo of Teilhard de Chardin en famille

In those old sepia photos,
family arranged like statues,
you may note one child
who stands apart with a solemn face,
stares in a different direction.

That one will go off,
never return.

Perhaps from war.

Like my uncle Ivan,
beyond the edge of clustered
siblings and cousins
in *"La famille en pique-nique,
auprès du Baltic 1911,"*

before he filled notebooks
with passionate novels,
was shot to death at nineteen.

Or like one daughter who won't
look at the camera or smile,
takes to the road,
neglects postcards.

She may try to peddle poems
on the street, or the sounds
of a clarinet, a canvas
preserving familial blood
in smudged fingerprints.

Often they give everything away.

If they were to come home,
hands empty, scarred,
try to fit themselves back
inside the frame among siblings
and litters of nephews and nieces,

their eyes would glow
with prodigious visions —
char the paper,
splinter the frame,
smash the glass —

HIBISCUS CHILD

for Alexander, born on Cyprus

Hibiscus hedges crimson and salmon
encircled your birth on that hot island
where copper surf beat

copper rocks, turquoise waves curled
ephemeral as petals you grasped
in your miniature hands.

Midwives in snow-white gowns
like a ring of fairy godmothers
promised you beauty and brilliance.

They forgot to mention
fortune, fame, safe
journeys, or common sense.

Slighted by your beneficent witches,
still you blossomed...But now
you charge about on perennial quests,

scatter copper and gold
to fickle strangers,
bouquets to every girl,

while we stand by confused:
your trails of promises broken,
unpayable debts, and pain —

Far from you now in a snowy land,
I watch the hibiscus plant on my sill
swell into flowers, one every day.

Each lasts only a day. That flashy cycle
completed, rooted in silence again
the plant retreats into green,

like you changing mood with the season,
thirst never slaked, storing blooms
complex and red as our shared blood.

13

WHY SOME NIGHTS I GO TO BED WITHOUT UNDRESSING

*(For poets Josephine Jacobsen, Rod Jellema, Irene Rouse,
Roland Flint, Barri Armitage, and David and Judy Ray,
who lost sons and a grandson in automobile accidents)*

Even as my children scale
jungle-gym and pine,
they too are swinging toward silence.

In desperate dreams I try to save
my daughter from the flood of night.
Still she drowns and drowns

while both my sons
spin nightmare wheels
against a thundering sky.

This wet midnight terribly awake
I pace the living room. My youngest son
is driving his broken Toyota home

from The Grateful Dead Live In Concert.
The storm keeps pouring over icing streets.
Finally I go to bed

but toss, alert for doors or else
strange strained voices on the phone,
and I do not undress.

14

MY DAUGHTER BORROWS TWO EGGS

To feed her new lover
œuf à la coque
with a rose in its mouth...

At a long-ago breakfast
my father explained to my lover
the symbolism of eggs:

"Fertility, hope, and perfection.
In gilded domes atop Russian churches
the Holy Trinity rolled into one."

What if, when the bells ring so hard
at midnight on Easter,
gold cupolas hatched into mystical roosters?

My father, ill and en route
to that perfect elliptical void,
has trouble spooning his morning egg.

Yet how much he could tell
of the liquid ovoid of loving,
fragile shells.

Still, today he bequeaths
to his waiting granddaughter
perfection, fertility, hope,

a remembered triad embedded
in two speckled X-Large eggs
with golden yolks.

FLYING TIME

"He asked me to fly to Bangkok with him,"
giggles the nurse. I picture my father's
wheel chair sprouting aluminum wings,
his skeletal shoulders growing feathers —
scarlet, vermilion, green —
like a swan sired by a parrot.

"I hope you agreed to fly with him,"
I answer. "He was a famous explorer."
She laughs, slaps her plump palms
against her white uniform.
"Lord, what a spaced-out
i-mag-in-a-tion your daddy's got!"

His blue eyes watch us. I smooth
wisps of hair like down on his skull.
My mad daddy...Here are
the springs of my imagination.
At eighty-four may I too
have license for madness.

Meanwhile I wheel his chair
to his place at the table
between old Mrs. Silverman
screaming "Sugar! Coffee! More milk — "
and Muggsy sloshing soup on his neighbor.
I set the brakes, fasten his seat belt.

Although my father insists that this trip
he would rather have curry and beer
or smoked eel and vodka,
I spoon pureed liver and unsalted limas
into his mouth quickly before
his fingers explore the plate.

◆ ◆ ◆

Downstairs, in the Ladies Room,
by mistake I enter the oversized stall
with handrails, high commode
and the blue-and-white "Handicapped" sign.
But will there be space enough here
for my wings?

GREAT AUNT ELEANORA DEFENDS HER DECISION
TO REMAIN ON HER FARM, ALTHOUGH AT NIGHT
OF COURSE THERE ARE SOUNDS

Most, I identify: from the woods, the hoot
owl; from the cove, loons;
scratchings, shrills, chirps in the roof;
wind spiralling down three chimneys
each with a singular moan;

and when I pry rot from a window frame,
the squeal that freezes against the pane
is explainable. But it's the voices the farm
absorbed over three hundred years —
from Indian plaints to quarrels over crochet.

Just now, among spindly figs, blackberry bushes,
runaway roses the farmer curses,
hawthorns which split the flagstone floor
of the shack burned in the Revolution —
who knows which side lighted the torch —

I noticed a child in a dark pink pinafore,
plump, about three, crying, nose running,
she had a cold, or was cold —
hard to decipher. Then, she went silent,
was gone. Or, was never there.

When the garden is ploughed each March
always in the rut near the broken pipe
which led to the barn — stalls still lettered
SMOKEY, STORM KING, OLD JESS —
I find one tattered rag doll.

I've settled in with the presences now,
woodchucks in the cellar, wintering mice,
piebald cats who meowl past the barn
their untamed ancestors guard.
My voices too will merge with the farm.

18

BREAKING FORMATION

Great Aunt Eleanora packs
her crusted palette with chipped plates,
blackened silver, tattered towels.

She piles shoe boxes marked
Zippers, Shade Pulls, Fuses (Blown),
Sheep Skulls, Arrowheads.

Neighbors mothball, roll the rugs,
pile split mattresses, sprung chairs.
The mice within resettling,

all is stored in two back rooms
as if she were just off
to Florence until spring.

Muslin shrouds her canvases
stacked for cut-rate galleries.
Paints dried to stone are thrown away.

Bags for Charity hold button shoes,
velvet dresses, splattered smocks —
someone might find a use.

Still time before the van arrives
to hobble past her untilled fields,
the barn where she hid out to paint,

the lighthouse on the bluff.
Below, where cove and sea collide,
ten mallards wait around a broken skiff

to gulp her scattered crusts.
Erect between her canes, she checks
the farm one final time, dry-eyed

until nine whistling swans — so close
she feels the brush of wings —
fracture the sun in a broken formation.

VISITING HOURS

Great Aunt Eleanora counts the pearls
that she no longer wears,

Great Uncle Ramsey checks his toes
amputated years ago.

Now you catch yourself adding up
your weightless pocket change.

Just as they spend hours plucking lint
from their stained dressing gowns,

and raise imagined food to toothless mouths,
you also find your actions void

while you look for omens, hope
in gestures of whomever else you meet.

No longer are you
merely visiting.

ASSOCIATIONS EN ROUTE TO A BONE SCAN

Bone...bone...bone...Desertscape
with deadwood, pebbles, scattered femurs,
tibias, with luck a skull, even fossilized.

A Ghanaian lady over lunch taught me to eat a chicken
properly: chew the cartilage, crack and split
the bones, suck the marrow, leave splinters.

Great Aunt Eugenya was a nurse in World War One:
when all four doctors in the unit died, she performed
amputations in the field. Thanksgivings here, only she

could carve it right...Doctors send small-boned, fair-skinned,
red-haired patients in for imaging. My skeleton, once strong,
designs the shadow of itself on screen...So far I have

consumed myself to 69% of me...Now everywhere I notice bones:
in soup pots, pet stores, butcher shops, battlefields.
At the Smithsonian: tyrannosaur jawbone, alligator spine,

kneecap of a kangaroo. Snake skeletons strung up like mobiles
rotate, float in bone-dry air. Back home: dog bones, their own,
and those they claim. Will enough of mine be left to chew?

A QUESTION OF BONES

Suddenly our own.
A hip here, shoulder
there. Fingers, toes
snap like icicles.

Gravity-cheating
trapeze artists before.
Now, bones airy as birds',
we can't lift off.

This elegant pelvis
which served so well
tilts toward
sagged ribs.

Our ingenious
skeleton
assembled with
transcendent cunning

from a personal
primordial stew
without our
collusion

brashly disjoints,
dissolves
like jellyfish
in tropic sun

or trickles
grain by
calcic grain
back into the pot.

LIKE MY AUNTS

Like Aunt Maria beyond Leningrad, at eighty-four
I shall live on a heel of black bread
and cucumber slices, intending to haul myself up
to boil the kettle for tea, while I wait

for pastries with poppy seeds, my murky eyes
seeing gold onion domes against indigo skies,
instead of burnt barracks across the lane
through blizzards of snow or bullets,

and, humming Tchaikovsky, I'll rarely allude
to deportations, the Siege, or children and dogs
lost to artillery shells, famine,
the stewpots of neighbors.

Like Aunt Jean who died at sixteen, overdosed
with morphine when she fell from her horse
(and she was "the beautiful one, the talented one",
while my fat mother clung to her fugues),

I too dream: center stage, when I've memorized
every part in every Shakespeare play as Aunt Jean did,
with Sarah Bernhardt, who attended her school performance
in Kansas City, Missouri, out there clapping, clapping...

Like the aunt I invented, I'll spend old age
painting medieval murals on crumbling walls,
while twenty-five cats mill around
and social workers bang and bang at my door.

My powerhouse aunts, unaware of your legacies,
all you asked of slippery fate was to live to the hilt.
I drink to aunts who will drop their knitting, kick off
galoshes, slip on dancing shoes or hiking boots,

perhaps use too much rouge, black lace trailing
beneath the hem, a cigarillo thrust in their lips,
and a slug of blackberry brandy poured in our tea —
Oh, aunties!

II.
FURTHER LEGACIES

GHOSTS

My grandmother at sixteen inherited land
south of Moscow, a stone manor house.
After the deed was signed, the family

retired to their rooms. She bolted windows
and door, fell asleep, her two borzois stretched
on the threshold. Suddenly in the night

she screamed and screamed, "An old man is here!
Covered with blood!" Servants broke down her door.
None of the peasants doubted her word.

The first landowner, cruel to his serfs,
had beaten one to death. The judge merely fined him.
As he drove home through the birches,

peasant women ambushed his troika, fell on him
with flails. He had died in that room.
His ghost appeared to every new heir.

◆ ◆ ◆

After the Revolution, during the Civil War,
my father lay wounded and ill from typhoid
in a monastery near Kharkov, when Ivan,

his missing brother, appeared and said:
"I was killed on the battlefield, but you
will survive, go where English is spoken."

◆ ◆ ◆

My father was always the only one
still awake downstairs
in our brownstone on 95th Street

when the ghost of a previous owner
ascended the stairs. My spaniel
Snuffy also would see him, and growl.

I was all by myself in the house
when Snuffy observed him climb
four flights to my attic room.

◆ ◆ ◆

Ivan returned when my father, aged eighty-four,
lay alone in a nursing home in Virginia.
He told me he knew why Ivan had come.

◆ ◆ ◆

My grandmother's ghost has visited me only once.
My parents have not yet reappeared
though they still haunt my pages.

Of late, every year or two, I hear that another
old lover has died, so far without violence
and in some other town, no time for farewells

or returns. Still, I'm fearful when you, my final love,
are not sleeping beside me in this old house.
And what if you should go before me?

IN THE ARCHIVES

Frayed pages, scratchy maps, half-baked campaigns.
Browned photographs: soldiers with antique rifles
defend the mud of the trenches,
visiting princes inspect old cannons,
anonymous prisoners slog through towns
with unpronounceable names...

Suddenly: my grandfather's picture!
The governor general of captured Galicia.
Posed beside the Tsar's portrait,
he wears his gallery of medals,
moustaches trimmed for the camera,
the dust of battles scraped from his boots.

He stands soldier-straight.
He has won the love of his troops,
the respect of the foe, envy from peers,
gratitude from prisoners and refugees.
He fought a number of hopeless wars,
survived a court martial with honor.

He is brilliant, foolish, on good terms with God.
But it is 1915. He will not govern for long.
Both sons will uphold the family name
on shifting battlefields.
One will die fighting with valor,
the other, wounded, will thrive in exile.

He will not abandon his damaged land
despite war, revolution, famine, jail.
Banished to distant cities, his ruined heart
will fail. Books recording his deeds will be
lost or banned, later revived, facts distorted.
Meanwhile, he reviews his troops in the archives.

AIDE-MEMOIRE

For Czeslaw Milosz, poet in exile

The great blue heron skims low
over the soy bean field
stripped by the harvester.

The lance of his neck probes wind.
Wide wings flap with languor
as if slowed by December.

He rises above bare hawthorn,
wineberry canes enclosing the pond
like barbed wire. If you saw him

you would recall the storks
on village roofs of your childhood,
your losses would flood over you

like tide in the marsh. The heron soars
over battalions of cattails, to the river,
disappears beyond channel markers,

but flings his shadow on furrows
where dried stalks bristle and
leftover velvet pods still hold seed.

VISITING GREAT AUNT EUGENYA BY THE CHESAPEAKE

Early each spring, I visit her
under the tall blue spruce, yank the first
shoots of pokeweed, honeysuckle and berry briars,
without disturbing the cardinals' nest.

In April her nearly blind eyes
could still distinguish the blaze of azaleas,
and she was always surprised
to have made it through one more winter.

◆ ◆ ◆

She'd dictated her will while we sipped
blackberry wine from jelly glasses: "Cast
my ashes into a garden..." Then,
with her elfin smile, "Also into the sea."

We drank to her ninety-first year.
How fiercely her fingers gripped mine
that May afternoon as the strange
dry gargle churned in her throat.

I'd just rented a farm near the bay,
was still setting in asparagus roots.
I dragged out the canoe, scattered half
of her off the island where tides run strong.

Then I took the trowel, dug in the rest
under the spruce which stands alone
at the edge of the farmer's field.
Several times a summer I cut back weeds.

His combine roars by like a tank as he
harvests his wheat, soy beans and corn,
the last row so close he grazes the boughs
unaware she's here in his sandy soil.

◆ ◆ ◆

In World War One, on Russia's wavering
battlefields, she nursed the wounded, signed
the cross over the dying…How many unmarked
graves fertilize that black earth…

After the Revolution, the Bolsheviks seized
her family estate for one more kolkhoz.
She worked as a nurse in a prison camp,
later escaped by train to Estonia, then

a place by a German lake, with pines.
The Nazis took it in World War Two, made her
manage a farm with *Ostarbeiter*, slave workers,
under their rifles in Poland.

Tiny, thin as the prisoners, she shielded them
from the guards, shared her own rations.
She led the horses, steered the plough,
planted and dug potatoes by hand.

The Nazis retreated, the Red Army advanced.
She hitched up the horses, piled refugees
in her cart, trekked West, caught a boat,
settled at last in a Washington flat.

◆ ◆ ◆

I imagine her fragmented heart
nourishing this singular spruce,
while blackberries sprout from her fingers,
chanterelles from her skull,

reassured that part of herself
is planted in terra firma although
another portion will travel forever,
flutter kicking through foreign waves…

◆ ◆ ◆

Now I must move on. The farmer already
ploughs my asparagus under. Will he think
to clear the pokeweed, honeysuckle and briars
before they entangle her spruce?

32

FLUTTER KICKING THROUGH FOREIGN WAVES

"But all waves are foreign."

— *Suzanne Collins*

Foreign, even those that fill, refill
tidal pools pocking this familiar beach,
this trickster mind, twisting algae strands.

Yet ripples do not really move, insisted
the physicist, molecules of energy just leap
in place. Jacks-in-the-box of a pond?

The unknown cat who squeezed through my door in Provence
one night, curled in the crook of my knees, emerges
years later and still unseen from my cot in Melaka.

A man encountered in one jungle
reappears in another, oceans, decades away,
bent beneath the same ponderous pack.

Everything becomes foreign and terribly close
inside the distressing cauldron of the skull
where loved and might-have-loved are twin.

THE WINE-DARK SEA

Moscow, Mid-July

"Summer is not my time to write,"
she shrugs, and obliges guests
with smoky tea, Armenian cognac,
her old poem about Homer.

The table glows with apricots,
glistens with gooseberry jam.
Curls of chocolate feather
the gift of an almond torte.

Then from her broken balcony:
a colder breeze invades.
A turned leaf blows across the floor
like a scrap, or a word.

Suddenly she lines her books like troops,
rakes wrinkled pages from a drawer.
Guests exchange glances, rise.
She does not detain them with chatter.

On his stormy wine-dark sea
Homer could not know
such brutal change of season.
Homer did not fear

a black car stopped by the gate,
nor men in grey overcoats
entering the courtyard. At times
we must all become blind.

ON THE RED ARROW EXPRESS

Moscow to Leningrad 1988

Imagine if I had been born among birches
and barricades, gold domes and gulags,
in this dangerous land, familiar and strange
from childhood, first seen now in a luminous

Arctic July...Whom would I have loved?
Would you have appeared on this train
at this hour, would we have known
how to speak with each other?

Would my hedonistic rebellious nature
be tempered by merciless winters,
unseasonal famines, eternal threats
of prison and wars?

In a 1942 photograph of the Siege
women are digging an anti-tank trench
or a mass grave. One girl lifts a spade
heavy with rubble, smiles at the camera.

Cheekbones wide, eyes too close, untidy curls.
Rib-thin. My double, age ten. A cousin?
Did she survive the Blockade? Would I have?
The train rockets on between cabbage fields...

CORRESPONDENCE WITH A RUSSIAN SAILOR

"Why do we worry so much about the words, the meanings
when they've done so little for us?"

— *Margot Trietel*

What a decade of letters I've sent
to Piraeus, Naples, Hong Kong, Istanbul,
Singapore, Panama, Havre, Bombay,

an atlas of foreign ports
fragrant with cinnamon, seaweed,
petroleum, coal dust, fish.

Your ship lands, you rush down the gangplank —
Guards challenge your passport.
Vendors, bartenders, girls intercept.

At last you find the POSTE RESTANTE window —
Surabaya, Yokohama, Rio, Marseilles —
"No mail for this name? Look again..."

And you post your flimsy envelopes stamped
with vermilion fishes, indigo moths,
portraits of local heroes.

Our letters get lost between salutation
and dock. Still we write until lines
scrawled on pages etch in our faces.

We scribble on water, on fog,
the shoulders of dolphins,
hummingbird feathers, cicada wings.

Danger needs no spelling out.
When one rare note arrives,
sentences catch in the screech

of cables round winches, words rush
with hawsers through chocks,
tear in the din of derricks and bells.

Gulls mistake flutters of shredded letters
for bread. Kisses XXX-ed in black ink
trickle like precious fresh water

into the languorous suck of salt waves
around pilings and hulls, while tide
lowers tons of metal and men

toward the muck of the harbor floor,
layers of sunken ships, driftwood, tires,
shells, exoskeletons, bones.

Amid jetsam of ocean and land
meanings hide, you disappear...
And still we write.

LETTER FROM BELGRADE

When I write the word *duška*— darling — here,
a tiny *v* must alight on the *s*,
a *v* like a bird perched but
wings spread, eternally landing
or taking off from the *š*
with a *sh sh swoosh*

merely pausing in full swoop
atop the serpentine *s*,
like an eagle diving to snatch an eel —

So you grasp me.
So you will fly away.
Bird, bird,
I scatter my crumbs to keep you here...

Duška. Duška. Duška —

IN THE BALKAN HOTEL

On the prickly red plush
of the Balkan Hotel
I wait for your call.
Like cries in nightmares,
it can't reach over oceans,
cross barbed wire.

I meet Mr. Abdul Hamil,
Sea Captain, Alexandria, Egypt,
ship due in Varna, Black Sea,
not until Sunday.
He invites me to lunch,
supper, and dancing.

We both know sepulchral hotel
meals alone, the shiver of icy sheets
beneath brocade spreads,
the echoes when radios listen,
and midnight thirsts. He snatches
the tab for my Turkish coffee.

I give him my map of the city,
mention the melon and fruity wine
ripe on my window sill,
but insist I am busy for lunch.
And perhaps by tonight
your call will come through.

SARAJEVO

1. June 1914

The Archduke is being driven
from manoeuvres
to the gala lunch.

The shuttle shoots
to the selvage
on hundreds of looms.

A watchman dreams of figs.

The plausible trajectory
has not yet met its mark.

Skinny ghosts spin
from the strings
of the village fiddler.

A cadet at attention too long
sways in the sun.

A shopkeeper counts
his coffee beans.
Flies land in bowls
of honeyed milk.

Heat and dust and blood
rise from the quays
in a furl of mosquitos.

2. October 1979

Rain slides down
entire horizons
of onion domes,
washes spires
in darkening tears.

Cold slips inside
thin coats,
soaked shoes.

Unquiet mud oozes
over bald cobblestones,
hides shadows
of old footprints.

In the riverbank park
snowberries glow
death white.

Parapets are decked
with maroon petunias,
velvety but

the bridge is too
narrow to bear
all that history.

Magpies stalk
the wasted river
for minnows, flies,
and their own
warped reflections.

Downriver the waters
run red: perhaps effluent
from a textile mill.

Prayer unwinds from a minaret.
Tombstones crowd
within cracked walls
and rusted grilles.

In a shuttered apartment
a battered trumpet
and accordion
attempt a minuet.

On these windy quays
I also wait
at a crossroad.

Had Gavrilo Princep arrived
in this colder season
his fingers might
have shivered too much
on the trigger.

But there are always
other assassins.

POWER OUTAGE

Dark grips us the way
a starfish clutches oysters,
the black snake swallows wrens.

Although we know the wind
extinguishes, constellations
shift, how thick the dark,

enveloped we still strike
our tiny matches to a wick
and think to lance the night.

THE OLD BRIDGE, AFTER THE WAR

The bridge was not badly bombed.
Corpses caught in the piles
but the span again is safe.
Bicycles, cars, even trucks

clang across the planks. Women hurry
with buckets, children, clothes to wash.
Two mongrels who escaped the cauldron
steal down the slope to drink.

The river glistens and gives back
facades of gutted structures.
From the ruined spire, cathedral bells
skip like stones across water.

The arches of the bridge are joined
by their watery halves
and once more on the river banks
the circles are cleated.

THE TRANSPORT OF KLAUS VON Z.

Someone is always out to find us. We try to live
quietly on a remote continent. New documents support
a sudden beard, hair grown out, color changed, fingerprints
smudged, burnt whorls. Our weight doubles or halves.

We take safer names. Harder to alter the tongue
to master unusual diphthongs, unpredictable vowels,
consonants softer than our gutturals. Words emerge
faintly European, though locals cannot pin them down.

We speak only as much as needed for obscure jobs:
we repair shoes, patrol the subway or sewer, read
gauges in labs where SILENCE hangs on the wall,
or farm a mountain snowed in for months.

Check-out clerks banter with elderly men (we are
shapeless now, our potato faces puff or sag),
but we solve encounters with a polite look
of being late for a pressing appointment. We move

often, without leaving debts, or addresses —
a cinderblock flat or modest brick house amid roses
on streets called Candlestick Way, Fox Run, Dove Lane.
We mow lawns at dusk, shovel snow before dawn, let dogs

run in walled yards. Drapes drawn all day raise questions
but net curtains muffle the sun's prying rays, silhouettes
cast by treacherous lamps. The wife (if we have one, here)
is the figure at the edge of the picture window.

Scratched records of *lieder* repeat and repeat too low
to trouble the neighbors. We switch on the radio for Strauss
or Wagner. Not for news, too disturbing, the wars
too nostalgic. And always those spent women and men,

especially the black-eyed children, creep into even
our plainest dreams, forever crying, bundled into dark coats
for the train, then mute, naked. Bones glow all night.
Their ragged shadows attach to kids here who zigzag past

our door in pastel parkas and jeans, innocent of history.
We imagine running outdoors to throw them a ball.
"Come in," we shout, "we will carve wooden whistles the way
our grandfathers taught us!" Those grey men we now resemble:

in their ill-tended graves, may they rest in peace...And you,
always on our trail, won't you leave us in peace! We were not
to blame — There was a war on then, after all, and everything
happened years ago in a distant town whose name you could not

pronounce...Surely each of you hides secrets, your heads
resound with betrayals, commands that would condemn you in
court! The lines you write in your dreams also fall like a whip!
You snap alert to the stomp of boots, the hum overhead of a
plane...

III.
THE ARC OF THE SEER

MUDANG: THE SHAMANS OF KOREA

Albeit women and of the wrong caste,
in Korea, shamans are treated with honor.

They heal, prophesy, exorcise evil
spirits by beating on drums and gongs.
And they speak with the dead.

Here, poets have similar roles
though seldom believed or honored.

We beat the drums of our skulls,
whack the gong into the night,
write to dead fathers, lovers, children,

as if they might answer us,
as if we could heal any one.

SEER, SURABAYA

"You do not fear your death,"
the stranger says, though the only
danger comes from the moon,

from our love of life so vast
we could risk either love or life
as simply as eating another mango.

Lilies vibrate with fragrance,
geckos croak on the roof
tiles the shade of dried blood.

"And your life's at a crossroads now."
Beyond the garden, the intersection
strangles with pedicabs, soldiers, goats.

"A poet can read the future," he says.
"Perhaps not for himself."
His milk-chocolate fingers close

over my palms, clutch our poems.
Then he embraces me. A rare gesture here.
"Remember, you are not afraid."

He slips through the gate
leaving me warm from his arms,
shivering.

Beyond the walls:
the echo of shots, sirens,
howling of homeless dogs.

COVERT MATTERS, SOFIA

The palms of strangers
                    spill their secrets
                              before my greedy eyes

Suddenly here in a chill foreign town
                                   in my own hand
                                            new lines are
etched
Unexpected
          mystic crosses appear
                    beneath the head line

My inconstant heart line
                    doubles then splits
                                        charges across
the plains

Beneath the Girdle of Venus
                    which long has betrayed
                                                 my
sensual tastes

lies a shadow sister or ghost crescent
                              the books seldom note
                                        the singular
Arc of the Seer

In this country of Gypsies
                    only I
                    cannot decode my own fate

SOUL SEARCH

The black-and-white cat
settles into my lap.
Claws reknit my sweater.

He stitches me to the chair.
Now he's asleep, and I
have no pencil or book.

I'd get up, but remember
an ancient Malayan warning:
Do not move a sleeper.

While the body sleeps
the soul takes off, returns
only when time to awake.

Should the soul drift home,
discover the body displaced
how could the soul rejoin?

So the weight of one
now soulless cat
binds me to the chair.

I grow drowsy but must
stay awake in fear of where
my soul might meander —

NIGHT PEOPLE

How they roll in,
the dead,
crowding my night!

My father said, "If you dream
of someone you've never met,
it means that person just died."

But Father, my dreams
swarm with strangers
I never considered mourning,

I'm much too busy making
their odd acquaintance
under fragile conditions.

Familiar forms —
parents, lovers and friends —
also people my sleep.

Each night they float in
like swans, converse in phrases
insubstantial as down,

flutter feathery hearts
like torn kites caught on twigs
beyond that slippery wall.

I try to preserve them
in amber, formaldehyde —
"Stay!" I beg them.

"You've told me so little
or I was too hurried
to hear you out —"

But the sun
clips the wings
of sleep.

A DREAM OF SIBERIA IN APRIL

The death occurs
in one of those hamlets,
refuge of hermits and Doukhobors,

where the single path in
has been lichen and moss
for a hundred years.

A stranger stops
for one night in a hut,
gives no name.

Snow flecked with red
begins to melt
over the frozen mud.

Flies and mosquitos wait
under puddles of ice
to wing through leached air.

Soon the tundra will burst
in purple and yellow anemones.
The earth remains stone.

So the deceased
lies in the shed,
cannot be planted yet.

He leaves an unstrung guitar,
a patched coat, boots with holes,
a linen shirt with a monogram

no one can decipher. The lines
on his palms predicted
betrayal and danger,

broken stitches told wandering,
the curve of his arc —
a reader of dreams.

THE RESEARCHER SENDS OUT A CALL

Sell me your dreams, in particular
dreams about roses, stags,
silver pitchers, whatever they hold.

Show me your palms, especially
those lines that net us our loves.
That's what I'm after,

when you strip the fur from the deer,
the petals from flowers that only bloom
in speckled dark behind your eyes,

or you drain the potions to tame
your lovers and foes. I need those hands
to spin my own cat's cradle of dreams.

UNSCHEDULED FLIGHTS

*"In the dream we will examine, one of the authors has set
fire to Logan airport in Boston and becomes filled with a
feeling of exhilaration."*

Minstrels of Soul: Intermodal Expressive Therapy,
Paolo J. Knill, Helen Nienhaus Barba, Margo N. Fuchs

The airport is burning its way through my dream
where we stand on runways eating tiny packets of peanuts,

washing them down with undersized cans of juice —
orange, apple, tomato — and sodas warm from the fires.

Planes move from hangars as if the pilots
lay slumped on the brakes bathed in molasses.

Cold coffee leaks into panels bristling with spinning knobs.
Dials shiver, lights flash, sirens spin lariats of warning —

Swallows dart from the tower enveloped in feathers of flame —
All controls OFF, everything slowly explodes —

lounges, ticket counters, news stands,
security gates, X-ray machines, wash basins —

Only the carousels with lost baggage
continue around and around, waiting

56

RED DREAMS

He fights muggers, vampires, assassins.
By morning his pillow is spotted with blood.

Some nights, it's only a mild knife fight,
barely a trace remains. Last night a duel — with whom?

Today his pillow is soaked and torn, feathers darkening
vermilion as if the chicken were just sacrificed.

He can't recall details but it was more
than butchering birds or deciphering entrails.

Kosovo, Waterloo, a terrorist bomb,
or a fratricide poorly disguised.

Whatever, I peel off the pillow case.
The ticking, patterned blue flowers,

is now ripped and the background red
like a color negative of the lawn.

I soak the bedding hours in bleach,
rinse well, hang in the sun to dry.

But how do I clean all these feathers
still floating throughout the house?

ANISE

To ward away
bad dreams,
insects,
age,
mice
and the Evil Eye,

the book says: tie
pimpinella anisum
on the pillow,
chew the licorice seeds,
and wear the yellow-white
bouquets to bed.

I do.
Even so
my pillow harbors
nests of mice
who scatter petals
of anisette,

bugs hover over
the coverlet,
I gnaw
the licorice
of nightmares
until dawn,

and whenever
I awake
I notice you
in spectacles
studying
my changing face.

KAYLIE READS MY CARDS

For Kaylie Jones

The Sun turns face up, radiates
gold spokes across this strange

portentous game of solitaire.
My queens look pensive, satisfied

the emptied cups are left behind,
henceforth my chalices are full.

Long labors with the chisel lead
to every stave in bloom,

pentacles now heaped
like pumpkins by the gate,

happy travels to and over water,
the marriage bower blossoming —

But again the Fool is poised
above the precipice,

and that fat old Devil wears
his tail on fire, like mine.

WARNING SIGNS

Poison ivy grows under my lettuce.

Should be the end line, not the first.
An omen that lasts
long after words, or rashes.

Warnings are meant to precede:

*Avoid alleys. Death lives
in the medicine cabinet,
murder under the sink.*

*Germs lurk in your dishrag,
microbes multiply
in the mayonnaise.*

*As for that mountain, remember: what
goes up, comes down, often head first.
And it's a mile to the ocean's floor.*

Even those lofty precautions fail:
Who says safety pins are safe.

A child can re-assemble a gun
better then you, who haven't the patience
even to wait until the light changes.

The skull of the wild boar I found
beneath a feathery casuarina tree
stares down from my study shelf

as if his eye sockets were full
and I were succulent.

DOOR STEPS

for Katherine Govier

But there's always some blind
piano tuner knocking and knocking;

or the plumber one week overdue
now in a wheelchair waiting
for you to maneuver him up and over
your threshold, three hundred pounds,
and tuck a damask napkin under his chin
so he won't spill the soup;

or a child with palsy
soliciting for Special Olympics;

a pair of insistent witnesses
to the Kingdom of God
in white shirts;

or only an abandoned cat
who knows better than you
how to get on in the world.
You are part of his plan.

Of course it might be the rapist
who's tried every house on the block.
You are the only lady at home
mid-afternoon in your negligée
so won't you please let him in.

Whoever, you can be sure
they will come knocking midway
through the wrong day, sensing
through layers of brick and wood:

However disheveled,
sooner or later you will
answer your door.

RAZORMAN

He picks up my single-edged razor,
the one I use for clipping news items,
and we circle the table in an odd dance
of — fear? Desire?

Not someone I remember
outside this dream
yet not total stranger within.

Six-foot-four with black pompadour,
not quite my type, a bit slick.

Still, I may have invited him in
for tea or a scotch. He is wearing a tux.
Has he followed me home from a party?

He seems to know me, insists
he wants to know me much more.

This is no way.

He draws blood —
quick swipes of the blade
so sharp I hardly feel pain —

Merely one of those nightmares
after rich lobster and chocolate cake?

Tonight I come out alive.

But when in the morning
I can't find that blade,
I do not replace it, take care
to lock up my manicure scissors.

IV.
LATITUDES, ANTIPODES

READING THE STONES

I watch for rocks
to guide me along
perilous journeys:

a configuration
of balanced boulders
on a cliff above
dangerous straits,

inukshuit, humanoid
cairns created by ancient
Arctic Peoples to mark
a way through blizzards,

or a certain shape
of granite ridge
silhouetted against
the carnelian sun,

a natural heap
of debris spilled
by an avalanche

warning: beware
gravelly slopes
and trying to climb
too high.

On a cold beach
I inspect
scatterings of stones,
try to decipher

jasper and agate,
quartz shot through
with serpentine,

glassy obsidian,
and speckled pebbles
glistening with mica.

I pocket the gray
stone ringed with
a perfect white circle.

EN ROUTE TO THE MORAL REARMAMENT HEADQUARTERS

I am climbing the mountain to Caux.
There, my Quaker teacher Miss Smedley said,
I will learn to reform the world

and, mostly, repair my soul:
just heed the testimonials of those
who have found the right road.

Age eighteen, a pilgrim sent to do penance,
I start up the twisting path from Montreux,
toward the frown of the crumpled Alps,

up the goat-steep mountain above
Chateau de Chillon half in the lake.
Last night beneath the full moon

I picnicked beside those stone walls
with the handsome pre-med from Missouri.
Hundreds crossed that moat only one way.

We talked of Plato and Sartre,
and managed not to let
anything happen again.

Still, at dawn I start toward Caux
not in sneakers or hiking boots
but sandals, my toes all air.

I hike away from the town's trapezoids,
higher above the shrinking fort,
Lake Geneva knitting up little boats.

As I round one more zigzag bend
a wind full of fruit
floats down the emerald slope —

My toes squash something wet.
Flecked as with blood I gasp.
Overhead, thousands of cherries!

I climb the tree, pick and eat
until I am purple-red,
ripe on the road to Caux.

TO RIDE THE WHITE CAMEL

Nefta, Tunisia

Wait in silence while all
the beige, brown and gray
camels lumber away from the well.

Wait in silence
on beige, brown, gray sand
until the white camel approaches.

She also waits.
Offer fresh dates
from the palm overhead.

If she accepts, weave jasmine
flowers into her bridle.
Lead her toward the rushing

channel of water
along the clay aqueduct.
Fill your amphora upstream.

When the white camel kneels,
grasp the pommel of olive wood,
swing up and over, onto the saddle.

She hoists herself up
like an earthquake.
Apologize for the burden.

When she stops in the pomegranate grove
reach for the rosiest fruit.
Split the skin with your nails.

When you reach the cactus fence
if the white camel wishes,
proceed into the desert.

Do not be certain
either of you
will return.

Continue across the Sahara
eating the pomegranate
seed by infinite seed.

GEOMETRY ON THE TORONTO FERRY

First, the angle of the child
who, braced against the slant of deck,
pulls against the pull of larger hands
which make a broader angle of their arms.

Then the flag, upper left, oblong
banner of the brave. The ferry crunches
ice ahead, her brief diagonal course
set across the port, and back.

The shattered rhomboids, triangles
of ice floes churning in our wake
freeze back into a solid plane.
The child strains toward the ladder

to the bridge, would grab that wheel,
steer our stolid trapezoidal craft
straight to Spain and — smash geometry —
he would prefer a brigantine.

SEVERAL MEANINGS OF COLD

for Pedro, Toronto, October

The kid from Mexico saws the dead cedar
to logs. He's newly arrived, and broke.
She needs the tree cut, spreads her hands
the width of the barren hearth.

"Win-ter comes in Oc-to-ber here," she enunciates,
shivering in the futile sun. She flutters
gloved fingers skyward as if the red-orange-gold
fallout of leaf flakes were icy white.

Has he seen snow in his mountains?
Or only soot falls from cities, volcanic ash,
the dust of drought? Perhaps blizzards
of russet wing flakes from migrating monarchs.

Here, he will learn several meanings of cold:
the cold, *how* cold, *a* cold, *cold* shoulder.
What of the ice of the muted voice,
deep-freeze of the heart...

She'll pass on her son's outgrown parka.
The grocer sells chilis, red-devil hot.
She thaws one can of juice. "Drink."
Should she offer hot coffee?

His notched blade grinds the resistant trunk.
She picks up a log, sniffs the maroon-pink core.
"Fragrant. Good smell. Log. Saw. To saw a log.
Two logs. Saw. See. Sawn. Seen. Seesaw. Say..."

How vital the shift of a letter or two.
Gusts whirl sawdust like beige snowflakes.
"Cold. *Frigo.*" She hopes that's correct. "*Frio?*"
"Wind. Cold wind. Win-ter. Win-ter. Cut. Cut. Cut."

71

MID-OCTOBER REPORT FROM THE ROOF OF THE WORLD

On my Northern roof deck, tomato plants
still press triumphant poisonous leaves
toward a brief sapphire sky. Their last
green stones must redden indoors.

A few trios of yellow florets, smaller
than honeybees' wings, dangle under
the branch tips, as if it were never
too late, despite frost warnings.

Farther north, the Innuits, Innupiaks,
Siberian *Eskimosy* in icebound hamlets already
pack in for the polar night: gallons of kerosene,
tins of tuna, sardines, baked beans, tomato sauce.

Will they ever see live tomatoes sprout
from flat freckle-shaped seeds, grow
into bushes swinging love apples,
pommes d'amour, pomodori, pomidory ...

But then, I've never known the Long Spring
and round-the-clock summer days, or made love
through a night that lasts months. Nor have I
yet tracked that Wise Crone who captured the sun

in her cat's-cradle-net, conceals it in a secret
igloo or glacial crevasse, limps out alone across
the tundra to die, knowing her soul will pass into ours
when we kill and eat the polar bear who just consumed her.

TERRA IRREDENTA: THE ELDER SPEAKS

For Rose Manning,
Ipperwash Army Base, Ontario

My birth string is buried
on this point of land,
my sisters' cords too.

And the youngest's bones,
our grandfather's skeleton.
He caught pneumonia

building this base: they
worked them hard, his clothes
were thin, the winter cold.

Our father died far away
fighting the war that was
why we lent you our land.

I was twelve when they cleared
this reserve. Now sixty-five,
my face like a walnut shell,

I have returned. Do not
tell me I'm trespassing.
This never was your land.

My sons, grandsons, stand guard.
Their pickups block the road.
Those years away in your world

we learned your ways,
learned to fight back.
Some learned to kill.

THEM

St. John's, Newfoundland

The leathered man hauling his mule,
the immigrant woman throwing slops at dogs,
the kid at billiards, his hands smelling
of fish or the scent of a girl...

This brutal blessed gap, as between two
arms of the harbor when even at low tide,
ice like dumped paving blocks,
it's dangerous to cross.

                       Certain nights
after too much sweet wine or poppy-seed cake,
we dream their dreams. We do not mean to,
we cannot wake in time to shut them out.

With the long reach of dead lovers, they
grasp our sleeves, scratch our skin,
snatch our pillows, leave us naked
on mattresses stuffed with corn husks.

The funnel blast that calls them back
to dory, barge or ship, we hear
miles from any port.
                 And their blood

matches our own, the murk
of their minds and lives seeps
into ours, as we try to ford
the straits, cross the ice in time.

KOREAN LANDSCAPE, 1977

for an estranged husband
who photographed
his battlefield for me in 1952

One plum tree
blooms again
beside the crater.

Patrols of pines
still bend and writhe
against a sky on fire.

Cranes and jets
fly through
the moon.

The landscape
has not
changed.

DISCOVERY: PERHENTIAN ISLAND, MALAYSIA

Only shattered cowries here,
unhinged scallops, amputated
coral fingers in the sand.

Suddenly: one thorny oyster shell!

Lower half inside is fluted white,
upper valve lips — russet striped,
spines lavender and pink.
Chipped and worn, yet hinged.

Within the shell I find
my brilliant drunken mother.

She found the only other
thorny oyster in the world.
Caribbean? Thailand? Nigeria?
One of her "better" days?

Her shell traveled wrapped up
with her pearls, sat on the mantlepiece
before the sea-worn wooden goddess.

My parents found the little statue,
jetsam from a wreck, on a Kamakura beach
the day they meant to separate
but confronted by this talisman
Buddhist and benign, stayed bound.

Her jewelry got broken, stolen, lost.
She pressed on guests whatever they admired:
her coral beads, amber pendant, blue pearl ring.

After parties, she'd pay a butler three times over,
while glasses, ashtrays, Grandma's best Limoges,
slid from her swaying tray en route
to the kitchen where a bottle hid.
Then, still dressed, she tripped to bed.

When she died, the hospital returned
gold ring, false teeth. They must
have thrown that dusty shell away
or movers broke it later on.

The goddess stands upon my shelf
though she can't salvage
my wrecked marriage.

I could not mourn her dying then.

Now, on this rough island off Malaysia,
as salt spines press like urchins in my palm,
I celebrate our perfect thorny oyster shell.

NOTHING, ONE APRIL EVENING, KYOTO

The painter was already drunk on cherry
petals he claimed smelled of death

yet he flung them in her hair
while they walked by the stream

discussing circles of ice, a pair
of unseasonal herons, the concept of *nothing.*

Now they kneel on a grass mat surrounded
by herons of mother-of-pearl.

Their hosts warn her,
"Go slowly, you are new to the game,"

still keep refilling
her black lacquer thimble,

then go off to boil rice,
heat more wine.

He admits his fear she might
kill herself. She demurs.

He bullies her into swallowing
another thimble of wine.

She looks in his narrow eyes suddenly
widening, watches him swallow her.

She would eat a red centipede
if he asked at this moment.

They eat each other's raw fish
with dark salty sauce and more wine.

He murmurs his hunger not just for food.
She tries to decipher what else he says.

He sketches on rice paper, rice wine
his ink to keep their secrets unseen.

He draws her into a white moon flower
then scatters her petals.

He turns her into a heron
and snips her wing feathers.

He makes her into a fish in his net.
The wine dries. She disappears from his page.

Just as well they know
their hosts will return,

ensuring the loss of nothing,
ensuring more hot rice wine.

TEATIME WITH MR. CHOY

for Wayson Choy

1.

A question
of Russian tea
or Chinese.
Black or green.
Compromise:

Czar Nicholas
in Canton cups
fragile
as eggshells,
translucent.

Desiccate leaves
uncurl among
wet butterflies,
peonies, illegible
calligraphies.

Paper flowers
unfurl from
cockle shells.
Dead lives rise
through steaming tea.

2.
Amid the blizzard:
kumquats. Exotic.
More bitter than sweet.
Twenty pits.

Simpler to peel
crinkly shells
off litchi nuts,
inside bite free

succulent white jade
from ovoids of mahogany,
and find our highs
in poppy seeds.

3.

The rip of a rag:
Childhood unfolds
from torn sheets
binding baby loins.

How to unshroud what
came before, the tear
from one, emergence
into another womb.

How to unravel
the whether.
How much new cloth
to blot old tears.

4.

My jade is a green
grasshopper,
a first-wedding
gift from Taiwan,

long in a drawer
of my rosewood
sewing cabinet
in another town.

Did the distant
giver with his
polished blessing
also try to warn:

Beware, girlbride,
the greening mind
may jump, glide,
soar, chirp, devour;

the body, exquisite
mechanism, seeming
stone, remains
insect ephemeral.

At last I leapt away.
Real grasshoppers
have compound eyes,
scan 360 degrees at once.

But wings fray,
tarsi stiffen,
spurs dull, eyes dim,
chirps turn laryngitic.

Yet legs bruised
by unplanned landings
on rocky soil, still spring
at the sun, wings fiddle on.

5.

At dawn

the squirrel
finds unusual seeds,

unfamiliar lines
appear on my palms,

new birds alight
on ancient scrolls.

IN HIS TIGER CAGE THE PRISONER OF WAR

Half-dead, he dreamed his childhood's cove, recalled
that possum caught in his chicken-wire crab
pot left above the tide line where he'd hauled
his skiff. The possum wriggled in the trap
lured on by smashed clam, fish head, chicken back
mouthed bare by minnows, now dried up. Their scent
still clung along the smaller bait cage tacked
inside the wire cube. Once through the vent
no way to crawl back out the jagged throat
or force apart the top or pop the latch.
How long had she hunched there beside his boat,
claws hooked to airy hexagons, the patch
of berries circling...How long must he wait
for some external force to spring his gate.

WATCHING TV FROM THE CHECK-OUT
IN THE FIVE-AND-DIME

Her miniature SONY reports: "Delegates meet today
in New York" — To repair the world?
A resolution not unlike one
approved months ago.
Still they can't solve — or dissolve — all the refugees
who keep fleeing, somewhere, or having fled

try to survive. [Now a docu-drama on birth.] I've fled
to the dime store today
quickly before my whirled
laundry completes its cycles. I must buy one
fuse: my dryer blew weeks ago.
[Melon-bellied lady on camera.] The cashier's a refugee

from Hanoi. We often talk. With seventy refugees
[TV commercial for Uncle Ben's Instant Rice] she fled
in a fishing boat. Many died of hunger, exposure, days
tossed on the China Sea, in a world
[Pampers commercial] where no one
offered haven. [Labor pains graphic.] Nowhere to go

but an islet abandoned decades ago
for lack of water. [Pepsi commercial.] 2000 refugees
camped on rocks, some gave birth, more died, all fled
Vietcong gangs, Chinese sailors, Thai pirates, Malay cops, days
of awaiting response from that world
beyond the simmering horizon. [Labor proceeds.] Then one

official called out the girl's number: someone
in America would adopt an orphan, she could go,
no more fighting for rice...My father, a young refugee
from a different revolution, fled
to America. [Push!] My shopping cart's full: White Sale today.
Her fingers punch the register. [Another birth swells the world

population, distracts the check-out line.] From around the world
items overflow onto the counter. [Push!] I forget the one
fuse. [Push, push — On TV now everything goes.
"Push," the nurse urges. "Push."] I think of refugees
pushed from shores, pushing for food. [Water's broke, OB's fled
to the lady-in-labor. "Push, honey, push — Happy Birthday!"]

The cashier stands riveted. In that overcrowded world
didn't she observe birth? This took minutes of airtime. I must go
home to my wash but they cut the cord and the new refugee from
                        the womb faces the camera, baffled.

REPORT FROM THE DISTRICT: TOXIC PROBLEMS

A used syringe is lodged
in trash at the curb. I'd
pick it up but there's blood.
I point it out to the cop.

Lady, you know this street.
Call Sanitation at 8 a.m.,
or throw it into that bin.
He drives on uptown.

An elderly man paws the bin
for leftover burgers
or half-cans of pop.
He might prick his fingers.

Even if I kick the syringe
down the storm drain, it won't
disintegrate like a tissue
in rain, but stay, like fear,

for a child downriver to find,
pass on germs, invisible, real,
for generations. I
should dispose of this.

My own child waits in the yard,
and my healthy lover.
As I hurry home, I wonder
how can I strengthen the fence.

I'VE NEVER WRITTEN A BASEBALL POEM

For Reuben Jackson, who has

I didn't even make
the seventh grade
girls' third team

substitute.
Still can't
throw straight.

Last Easter, scrub game
with the kids,
I hit

a foul right through
Captain Kelly's French doors,
had to pay.

Still, these sultry
country nights
when I watch

the dark ballet
of players sliding
into base,

I shout "Safe!
He's safe! He's home!"
and so am I.

V.
GARDEN OF EARTHY DELIGHTS

LILACS

Lilacs have bloomed here 200 years
though the house burned a decade ago.

Hedges divided the vegetable garden
and yard where laundry was hung

from the boisterous peony beds
people still come to admire.

I should cut the deadwood. Instead,
I bury my nose in lavender spires.

Generations of grandmothers burst
from the heart-shaped leaves.

Each has her tale of how he courted her
under these lilacs, their miniature

stamens glistening and pistils leering,
or how she played here as a child

while her grandma hung out the wash,
took in an apron full of asparagus spears,

and how, just beyond the hedge, a wolf lurked,
or a man exposed himself to her curious eyes,

so for all her life, and mine,
the fragrance of lilacs was not

handkerchiefs trimmed with lace
but shirt tails damp in the April wind.

RADISHES?

Raphanus sativus, family Cruciferae

By March 15 we sow them,
the weekend between snow and rain,
between departure of the geese
and return of ospreys.

We scatter tan round radish seeds
along with spinach, lettuce, peas.
Theory is, insects will go for radish leaves,
ignore our nascent salad.

And with this plundered plot
a battlefield all winter — barbed briars,
exploding burrs, lance stalks that mark
Jerusalem artichokes like mines in mud —

it's good to see those darkgreen pairs
of thumbnail seedlings break through clods.
Rabbits, deer and woodchucks nibble
spinach, peas and lettuce to the quick,

but like the bugs, ignore our radishes.
We can't. They're ready first. We yank,
boast about our robust Crimson Globes,
White Icicles like carrots bleached.

We replant, replant, till friends complain
our crop mid-summer burns the tongue.
Radishes, forgotten, double, swell to baseballs,
split, bolt, blossom lilac-white.

This June we planted Oriental Diakons guaranteed
to grow three feet in length, or depth.
By August, they dug in too deep for scrutiny
or harvesting, then disappeared.

We've had enough of radishes.
But next March, as programmed
at migratory birds, we'll sow
more *Raphanus sativus*.

CACOPHONIES

*"Drought-stricken plants emit high-pitched noises
as their cell structure breaks down, and scientists
are trying to determine if the sounds are attracting
destructive insects."*

—*New York Times, Sept. 4, 1988*

Unwatered, vegetables turn vociferous:
dill sighs, lettuce whines, peas pop,
cucumbers spit their own seeds with a ping.

Radishes argue in a dull
bump-bump-bump, an occasional
harrumph mistaken for a frog.

Potatoes, parched, grow hoarse.
Corn rattles skeletons of stalks.
Asparagus feathers shriek.

Bean tendrils scratch their poles
like fingernails on blackboards.
Chard snarls, tomatoes rage,

turnips growl, zucchinis scream,
watermelons bellow, rutabagas roar,
pumpkins boom, burst in a frenzy of seeds.

Gone mad with thirst
even weeds hardy in heat
put up a racket.

And, circling in formation,
lexicons of insects mass,
mandibles clicking, clicking.

MUSHROOM MERCHANT, KOREA

Old peddler on the mountain,
you offer what you call
mushrooms of immortality.

How can I be sure?
I ate toadstools once in Maryland
and nearly died.

You pat the basket on your back,
beg me gamble once again
with fungi pale as bones.

Do they phosphoresce?
Would I glow in the dark
for all eternity?

Mushrooms overflow my hands.

ON A REQUEST TO GATHER PUFFBALLS

For Eric Jacobsen, at 90

Yes, come October, after rain
we'll hunt those rotund fungi
like lumpy swans' eggs lost
in tufts of graybrown grass.

First we must climb a stile,
follow sheep paths through the meadow,
slither through barbed wire,
leap from log to rock,

ford the stream, cross a swamp
where ferns and orange jewel weed
hide quicksand on each side.
I will lead you up the bank,

through brambles, underbrush and vines
to groves of slender paw-paw trees.
Ellipsoid fruit falls applegreen,
purples, sweetens, underfoot.

We'll eat it quickly, spit the seeds,
sow a paw-paw forest, then
charge up the steep and humid slope
to sight the hundred-year-old oak —

Here, every autumn I discover
twelve puffballs huge as volleyballs.
A picnic for the Cyclops, or Goliath.
But each fall I've come too late.

Ivory flesh has rotted, browned.
Dust bursts through crumpled skin.
Nothing left to do but kick them,
scatter spores, at least ensure

a million more puffballs next fall.
Always only twelve appear.
But *this* October —

ANNUNCIATIONS, SEPTEMBER

While she waits, she gathers tomatoes,
eggs from the snowy hens,

plums from a seed
she planted at seventeen.

The sea smells of flounder and crab.
Her house smells of basil and yeast.

Spiders have woven together
the corners of rooms,

katydids whir emerald songs,
crickets sing in the cracks.

The younger man comes down the road
with a basket of peaches and wine.

One string hangs from her mandolin:
he winds it around the peg.

They cross the yard. Leaves spiral,
catch on zinnias, jimsonweed.

He bails the old boat in the sand
with the shell of a horseshoe crab.

High tide. They sail from the cove,
ignore squalls and the rising bilge.

All day his eyes speak
of desire and regret.

All night in the waves
she dreams: after years

a bright rush of blood,
new songs on the mandolin.

HARVESTIMES

In this season of pumpkin and frost,
one by one she drops off her lovers
from a broken farm wagon

to the false candlelight of taverns,
gaping cloacas of brothels,
the village inn.

The one whose bed she would share
this moonless night
has crossed other rivers.

Wagon spokes rust, turn
across fallen stalks. Wheels spin
in ruts between fields.

She lies alone upon a wide bed.
It yields narrow sleep.
All night she keeps watch

over unharvested souls.
Autumnal ghosts waver in,
torment her awake.

At dawn crows caw in her ears.
A castrated cat courts her cheeks.
Then, in the tangled garden,

she gathers the last green tomatoes,
buries plants singed by the frost,
folds herself into the earth.

PARINGS

The skin is tougher
on a yellow apple.

Eve pares his, wraps
the spiral around herself,

tosses herself otherwise
naked into the grass.

"Eat me," she says, then warns
apple seeds contain a toxin.

He shrugs, but his teeth
cannot pierce the skin.

Simpler to quarter but
he cores her,

eats the bared fruit
quickly before it browns.

WITNESS

Here comes Adam down the mountain
astride his onager! I crawl
from my thornbush to invite —

"Begone, old hag!" He pushes me aside,
kicks his half-tamed beast
toward the valley stream

where girls are bathing, our
daughters and granddaughters
too innocent and beautiful to wear

scratchy leaves and itchy hides
to shield them from the mirrors
of water and each other.

"Eve!" he shouts. "Eve?...Which of you..."
Terrified of his wild rheumy eyes,
girls scamper toward the cedar grove.

"Eve! Come back! Now where — "
"I am up here," I mutter, "you old fool."
He cannot comprehend that I have changed,

thinks I ran off with one of those
young bucks, our sons, grandsons,
who scrap among themselves like desert dogs.

Our hair is petal-white,
flesh like apples over-ripe,
teeth too sparse to test the latest crop.

My breasts hang baggy as a wild sow's dugs.
But how many suckled — Yahweh, we multiply!
I lost count beyond my fingers, toes.

Toes now too gnarled to walk. But my eyes are good.
I watch Adam free the onager to graze
while he crouches in the reeds.

He must be stalking fishes? lizards? doves?
His flint gleams in the sun.
Might he share his catch with me?

I always shared with him.
"Adam!" My parched throat cracks.
Wind blows my words away.

A young girl shimmies down an olive tree.
Like a lion Adam leaps
thighs still stronger than his mind —

Yahweh! He flings her on the moss!
"Stop!" I shout, "You can't — "
Her cries drown out my own.

I creep downhill. Stones cut my fingers, knees.
Horrified, I watch him mount
that child, lock himself into her.

His flint slits underneath
her breast, reaches through
her flaps of skin, saws through

the cartilage, the snap resounds —
He slashes his own chest,
opens that old cicatrice,

then inserts her borrowed bone.
As if it might take root,
sprout like a sapling in the spring!

He kneels, licks clean her blood,
tries to mask their wounds with clay.
And all the while, he moans, "Eve, Eve..."

The girl remains unmoving in her swoon.
Red berries glow beside the bank,
would quench my thirst.

He stuffs them in his mouth, and hers,
then yanks a crawfish from the stream,
tears off the claws, sucks the meat.

He whistles for the onager, grunts
how sore his joints, then pillows on
the beast and sleeps, appeased.

Ignoring dizziness and scrapes, I tumble
down the slope, reach that still form,
her face my own, before.

I wash her wounds, staunch blood
with plantain, comfrey roots,
garlic spears, marigolds,

then rock her in my bony arms,
sing mournfully until she wakes.
Sweet girl, I would explain,

the fault is mine, because *I am.*
But all she understands is
how she hurts, and where, not why.

O Yahweh! May whatever child in time
bursts through those loins grow up
to wield her head, her fists.

VI.
FAMILIARS

CREATIVE ACTS

I draw a stick.
The stick sprouts legs,
a head, long sleeves
that turn to wings.

An angel or
an insect now.

Did God know when
He started out
His would become
a man or bug?

ARS POETICA

My points of departure
are of manageable size,
common, quick to escape:

squirrels, raccoons, mice, bats,
of course cats and dogs (mostly
alleys and mutts), one wolf, bugs.

All soft to the touch,
my familiars, yet
innately wild —

that unexpected scratch or bite
will draw blood, leave scars,
might be fatal.

Someday when I've grown if not famous
at least big enough,
I'll tackle tigers.

Then the woolly mammoth, tusks
ivory sabers thrusting up
through ancient battlefields of ice.

NOT JUST ABOUT A SQUIRREL, OF COURSE

This is not right, is not
the time expected, so he
does not appear,

the mottled one with fur
turned from gray to winter ebony
so startling against snow.

Normally only mornings I put out
apple peels, pear cores, crusts,
a litchi travelled too far,
granola spilled and swept up
just for him,

gifts to appease for the oak
felled to make this deck
on the roof outside my room.

Between breakfast dishes
and plunging into my desk,
I pitch my rotten and stale
donations into the half-barrel
that will hold again next spring

one Big Boy tomato plant, marigolds
and weeds whose spindly bones
are all that poke through snow.
For now I call it the compost cask.

The instant I open the door
he vaults from the eaves surely
pleased — in an unfashionable
anthropomorphic way —
how well I'm trained.

He snatches his due, checks it out,
scurries up the rail, quick —
quick — he has a full agenda:

daily rounds of balconies and roofs,
bird feeders with imperfect foils,
fruitful bins in the park.

Monday I left a whole browned mango,
watched past noon as he tried
and tried to drag it off,
finally stripped it down
to the cuttlefishbone seed,

scolding even as he gnawed,
twitching, more irked than glad
for tropical exotica.

One must move fast,
weigh risks in a flash,
leap at times too far,
not trust too much:

I once roasted a squirrel
in my novel to save
the hero from starving.

In life I side step risks
and realities in many seasons
and venues, accept hand outs,
probe others' compost.

The tarnished pear, shrivelled plum,
are just part of the package
on the Day-Old Bargain shelf.
Squirrel is at the end of the line.

This afternoon I slip outdoors
with last week's half
of a cherry pie
nobody cared to finish.

Too soon it's dusk.
Now dark. Still no squirrel,
and the raccoon
who takes over summer nights
is hibernating in the roof.

Fresh snow already
hides my bribes.

Yet as I contemplate my
inevitable exit, so far
unwilled, a time when even
oatmeal is too rich to consider
and squirrels hide beyond sight,

I hope to be quick to this world
and my expectant feeders.

On the reverse trip
when no one, not even a rodent,
is watching, perhaps I
will put myself out for grabs
like a stale pie at the wrong hour
before the snow.

TOAD, SUNGAI KARANG, MALAYSIA

Each night I find the toad
come up the drain, cloacal
as his own interior plumbing.

He hops across the living room,
parks underneath my batik skirt
as if it were his jungle.

I don't disturb him, wait...
He does not metamorphose
to a prince, even minor sultan.

At dawn I capture him
with cupped hands, disappointment,
return him to the swamp.

By nightfall he will reappear,
his vernal croak proclaiming
more promises of transmutation.

Meanwhile he's live, catching flies,
avoiding snakes, sparking poems.
I too await a change.

GIANT CAMEROONIAN FROG

Now he hangs at the National Geographic Hall
like an abandoned diver's suit
or wrinkled dust-green tarpaulin
gone moldy a month in his jungle.
Size of a suckling pig.

He spawned upriver where waterfalls
cast rainbows over his skin. There
he snapped up bugs, lizards and snakes,
fulfilling their nightmares. Dark
drops early near the equator.

In my Maryland garden, toads
graybeige as drought, would fit
in a thimble, choke on an ant.
I turn the sprinkler on basil and dill:
clods spring into toads like thumbs jumping.

A copperhead glides into the spray.
We retreat, camouflaged among damp earth
and green feathers. Giant frogs crash
behind our eyes. We leap into sunlight again.
The snake leaves his skin like a shadow.

MARINE LIFE

Fish bob, belly topside, wash up until
the beach is littered with various species
shimmering, fat, even ten-pounders.

"Happens occasional summers,"
the watermen shrug. "Lack
of oxygen, no rain all month."

But I remember underwater explosions,
that naval airbase downriver
testing torpedoes or bombs.

Or something toxic loose in the sea?
Raccoons overprinted the sand
but left no mark on those scales.

Not one to waste, I take a stick,
push them out. Yet gulls ignore them,
or are already gorged. Carcasses float in again.

Rain at last. Even the skeletons
disappear. Crabs must have scavenged
until their carapaces burst.

Crabs might carry the germs of my own
destruction. Still, I'm a gambler, and hungry.
I bait all my traps, and wait.

FISH SCALES

They gleam all over the house.
You'd think I had flayed a tuna,
the 200-pounder hooked off Bermuda,

not a mere four-pound rock
still gasping for Chesapeake Bay.
My serrated blade scrapes scales

without scarring the skin: she'll bake
beautifully. Rosemary and sage
from the snowy yard. One lemon.

With each flying scale, she loses
her armor of mail, while I try
to become more hardened.

I dump spine, guts and roe for the gulls
and swans, who ignore this mess
like an afterbirth plummeting off the dock.

Since it's winter, the cove will stay
window clear to the bottom, until April brings
clouding pollen, scavenger minnows and crabs.

Scales glisten around the kitchen, scales
stick to strainer, dish drainer, soap,
scales decorate the lemon meringue.

Scales cling to the living room shag,
hot air vents, all three poinsettias, my hair,
the cable stitches of my best sweater.

Even folds of old love poems, and in bed
like finger and toe nails torn out
exposing nerves to the lightest touch.

◆ ◆ ◆

No matter how well I shampoo, vacuum, sweep,
like the fish bone stuck in my throat
each scale discovered months later recalls

those plated cheeks breathing in and out,
toothy lips moving even after I ripped
entrails away, severed her head.

EXPATRIATES

They chat between laps and dives,
two mermaids whom fishermen rescued from nets
and brought to the Health Club pool.

So many questions the mermaids can't answer,
and interpreters are scarce. No birth certificates,
passports or visas. Only their last residence is known.

The port authorities granted temporary asylum and advised
they apply for refugee or immigrant status if their skills
prove unique and they find long-term employment.

Hollywood sends scouts, talk shows adore them.
Impresarios flock with contracts, Olympic swim teams
would hire them to coach, owners of tropical discos

line up with lures of stereophonic aquariums.
Everyone wants to exploit their vocal aquatic talents.
They've auditioned their repertory: an *a cappella* recital

of dolphin whistles, whale songs, seal barks, swoosh of squid,
seabird calls, walrus grunts, rasp of the moray eel,
moan of the amorous octopus with whom they had a tangle.

They oblige interviewers with sea horse neighs
and sea mouse squeaks, the swish-lap-slap-smash
of surf against rock, and their own unearthly chants.

Intelligent beings, they've picked up some words,
though grammar remains beyond logic, gutturals catch
in their throats, *th's* stick in their teeth.

The Animal Rescue League, Amnesty International,
Greenpeace, Immigration, Welfare, the media
and six women's rights groups keep close watch.

115

So despite health regulations, and some inconvenience,
the club is pleased to give haven as memberships soar.
They freak out the clientele as they juggle dumbbells,

ride exercise bikes side-saddle, add a new twist
to push-ups, and slither under bleary-eyed swimmers
who rush off to office and home with unbelievable tales.

When the aerobics cassette blares, they dive in the pool.
Chlorine coarsens their curls, stings their eyes —
they giggled at goggles, tore off bathing caps —

but here at least there are no speed boats, submarines,
jet skis, nor unpleasant jetsam afloat on the waves.
Diet remains a problem. Vegetarians, they reject

tuna salad, sardines, salmon mousse, caviar.
The club provides pizzas, rice crackers in algae.
And they've discovered Doritos. But bulges appear:

they must swim extra laps, wrap caftans around
when they flipflop to steam room and sauna,
bounce on the water bed, nap on gym mats.

But the mermaids sleep in the children's pool
curled like seals on the white tiled steps,
pillowing on each other. And after hours

when lights are switched off,
their tears salt the pool.
They've learned enough words to ask:

"When can we return to the sea?"
The answer comes always the same:
"Too dangerous out there now."

So they wait in their borrowed harbor,
and yearn for ebb tide to turn,
for riptide, flood tide, tidal waves.

VISITATIONS, VIRGINIA CENTER FOR THE CREATIVE ARTS

What a flap when I gathered him up!
He can't fly yet though his wings
have dime-sized feathers, speckled and gray.
Shoulders and tail are tipped with white,
head is dandelion fluff.

I found him hunched by the garbage can,
this — mourning dove? — now on my manuscript.
But I can't let extraneous visitors interfere
with completing my work. I've already banned
six intriguing bugs from my study.

He hooks rosy toes over my fingers.
I should let him go — orphaned birds
rarely survive in a cage — but
the calico cat and ginger dog lurk outside,
no docile personae from nursery rhymes.

I have recovered evicted raccoons, squirrels
when trees fell, black snakes, the usual stray
cats and men. In Chapter Four I saved
one tiger cub, though the mother tigress ate up
my hero. Once I loosed a zoo on the town.

He ignores mosquitoes, beetles and ants.
He does not understand my sandwich.
I'm not up to pre-digesting a worm.
He clings to my shirt. Have we bonded?
I'd not intended…Yet don't we preach

the need to rescue remote refugees,
at least publicize their plight?
If you can't salvage the world, save a bird.
So, one more distraction: four ounces
of bone and down thrust on me

by fate or a storm or careless progenitors.
Might they yet retrieve their lost chick?
I lock up dog and cat, lower him to the grass,
retreat to my papers fragile as feathers,
and I keep watch.

STAYING AWAKE ON MOUNT SAN ANGELO

*for Richard Hill, who suggested
my film script needs a final rifle shot*

I.

An owl calls from the hemlock.
The moon is full.
My door flies open.

II.

Always that rifle
poised in the night
or first-light dawn
when visibility rides on the wing
of goshawk, skylark, crow.

If not rifle, a revolver,
an overlooked mine,
pit dug in the path,
sharpened stick,
flung stone.

Don't we need a hint of risk
at every curve of the spiral stair,
a mottled mirror to warn
the high and lovely cheekbone
is and will be bone.

III.

The train whistle spins
across the moon.
The deer lifts her head.

IV.

The shot that shatters
the pane in the night
might be a mistake

but who would come so far
in the heart of a storm
just to test his sights.

MAIL ORDER: "THE ULTIMATE SPORTSMAN'S KNIFE"

The traditional folding blade is etched
with "magnificent line art depicting
a majestic ten-point buck."

The handle is sterling silver engraved
with a repoussé stag and his doe
by a lake with the requisite mountain and pines.

Such a serene sylvan scene,
sibilant as the hiss
of arrows, buckshot or shell,

the swish of the blade as it flays
leather and fur the color of cattails,
punctures bladder, brain, illegible entrails.

The price of the knife is $195 (plus shipping).
The price of the life of the deer
is also probably high when you consider

transportation costs to the woods,
all the gear needed for life in the wilds
as well as weapons and ammo.

Pity a deer is not a gorilla or chimp
with the basic digital skill to turn
the tools of his or her own destruction

back on the hunter.
Pity a deer is not a tiger with teeth
or a charging rhino, elephant run amok.

You may return the knife to the Franklin Mint
within 30 days (presumably used is okay)
for replacement, credit or refund.

You cannot return the deer.
But it is indeed a magnificent knife
and would re-sharpen my pencil.

PASTORAL LETTER

for William Packard

Eight steers, not placid, move
with determination between
barbed wire and the briar woods.
All face one direction, the way
boats moored in a harbor keep
their bows to the wind.

I think of you whenever I see
cows in a pasture. For,
locked in your filthy city
with all its nervous excitements,
whenever I lure you to break out
you're turned on by bovine calm.

Can steers regret what they lost?
Over their heads, walnut trees
show yellowbrown leaves at the tips —
gypsy moths or cicadas?
Under the stony soil, grubs and moles
pursue their personal conquests.

And (steers, at least, can't
foresee this) the knife waits
until they have ruminated themselves
hefty enough. This may be also what
draws you to them: the shared,
after all, sureness of death.

SENTRIES

1.

October. Spiders
filter in, lace up
my windows and eaves,
would keep winter out
with fragile shadows,
dusty thread, needle
jaws, all those wire legs.

2.

Several snows into winter one spider
dangles against the pane, plain brown,
fat, belly a nickel size in diameter,
a dollar coin if you take in eight legs.

My anthropomorphism needs
no apology to imagine she sees me,
would like to come in, even switch roles.
Surely some flies I'd like gone?

They're long dormant. She should be too.
No business hanging on there,
no business banging against my pane,
no business in here to conclude.

Nor can I conclude with wrap-up wisdom like silk
or a web to capture, wrap up the situation.
All remains as before: spider outside, myself within,
eyeing each other, admiring, despising. Speculating.

Perhaps each will freeze as we are, in our place.

BEYOND LITTLE BLACK RIVER, MANITOBA

Snow crusts each birch and pine,
branch and log and stump.
The path is gone.

Suddenly a shake of winter-thickened fur —
a timber wolf.

I freeze as still.
We watch each other.
Snowflakes catch on eyelashes.

Do we both weigh our lives,
a final meal,
a fragile future of pursuit?

A tree cracks like a shot —
crashes —
avalanches snow —

In a flash we separate
toward different woods.

He will not lose his way,
nor point out mine.

THE PERSISTENCE OF BEARS

The bear continues to sniff our tent
though thirty years pass...

That hike, we spread our sleeping bag by the glacier,
surrounded by elk no one had seen all summer.

At midnight, after love, we watched the baby
raccoons scrape melon rinds lamp-shade thin,

then, reading Durrell by Coleman lamp
till I fell asleep, only you heard

the snuffles, snorts, heavy breaths warm
through the canvas flap, but did not waken me.

I'd not be frightened! That was the problem —
you knew I'd scramble into the starry night

to meet my first bear nose to nose, even
feed him the Oreos one by one until he was tamed

or swallowed my arm. So your purpose was prudence.
The start of a long censorship of what I should,

should not know, for my own good
and yours. Only, you did not factor in

those notorious maternal and uxorial instincts:
I sensed when the children began their experiments,

and foresaw, before you even fantasized, you
would embark on your own with the lady next door.

None of you lied very well, indeed told the truth
if I brought it up like a mistaken mushroom.

Meanwhile I learned to keep my own secrets
for your good, and mine.

COMPANIONS

That goose hides in your knapsack
cackling or venting an awkward honk
when you least expect.

You zip the bag, lace the strings tight.

A beak pokes out, long neck snakes around,
eyes gleam like hatpins, weedy breath on your neck.
Down clings to your hair like milkweed fluff.

And you could not kill her,
though you hint a taste for paté.

You hang your pack on an oak, slip away.

The goose wiggles out, lifts the strap off
the branch, and, as if mated for life,
waddles down the road after you, bag in beak
like an elderly lady lugging her purse,
day and night keeping watch, keeping you.

AFTER THE LAST NOTE OF A HARP RECITAL

At three I never pushed
an older sibling off
our piano stool
spun to its height.

No Mozart, though I
composed atonal sonatas.
I was branded bereft
of all cadence, tone deaf.

Yet aren't poets only
musiciens manqués: our
rhythms emerge in verse,
sonority in our words.

Lonely solos.
May my heaven boast
a full orchestra
with a HELP WANTED sign.

I will nudge
one harpist aside,
gently, without
ruffling wings,

sit on a cloud, pluck
forty-six catgut strings
and hope for angelic notes
as if these might appease

the souls of those felines
who've reached heaven unstrung
and must for eternity hear
how they've been recycled.

THE PEACEABLE KINGDOM

after a painting by Edward Hicks (1780-1849)

Will there come a time when tigers and lions
have eaten all those extraneous people camped
in their savannahs or plunged into their jungles…

They will be so fat from our plump flesh,
years may pass before they chase
zebras, antelopes or hares again.

Even lambs should be safe, for a while,
multiplying with such biblical fruitfulness
another good earth-cleaning will be in order:

Felines like a tidy universe.
Stretched across my desk, the tabby tom
awakes, inspects his claws, his teeth.

EARLY VERSIONS

Their larval stage is appalling:
six legs, or twelve, thirty-six, or unlegged
blind worms needing to feed and sleep.

So many successive moults:
split carapaces clutter the floor.
And all the itches they cause!

Regardless of genus or species,
untidy, greedy, incomplete, across
pasture and swamp they seek me out,

an attentive host, consider me mere carrier,
borrowed brain, rented womb, catalyst
to metamorphosis — *theirs*.

What a turn-off, these early drafts,
immature nymphs mincing as if prima donnas
already out there on center stage.

How cleverly they deceive me into conceding
they are ready to shake wet wings, flutter off, soar —
forgetting, denying their origins.

VII.
IN THE PEACOCK CAFE

BEDTIME STORIES

Begin with simple themes:
A milkmaid on her way to the stream
stumbles on a gold brooch. A princess
stabs her finger on a quill.

In the presence of his ministers
a king scratches mosquito bites,
a horse breaks from his stall,
charges over enemy terrain.

From then on, kingdoms crash,
winds howl down castle chimneys,
vipers emerge from the bath house,
there's a drop in agricultural statistics.

Or a tadpole swallows the brooch
without further metamorphosis,
the princess completes
her Ph.D. in herpetology,

the king goes fishing, the caught pike
plea bargains but ends up
in the *bouillabaisse* anyway,
and the king chokes on the brooch.

Suppose the milkmaid reaches the stream
for an assignation with the king,
but trips on the corpse of a cow, flees
and drops their baby into the marsh

where the gardener discovers and raises him
knowing when to prune a forsythia,
and the lad landscapes the palace, unaware
of royal genes but sensitive to mosquitoes.

However it starts, how to control it,
and why, or why not. Sunday mornings
in bed are especially fertile.
There's no telling what next.

IN THE PEACOCK CAFE

How many poets does it take to eat a croissant?

One to insist it be warmed,
then burn her tongue.

One to peel flake after flake.
One to probe the stiff underbelly.

One always searching the heart of every thing,
to plunge toward the innards, be disappointed.

One to complain of no butter or jam,
another to signal the waiter for honey.

One to flirt with the waiter.
One to invite him home.

One to dip a crust in a tisane
but not springboard seventeen volumes.

Another to wish he'd ordered a *Sachertorte*
and something stronger than linden tea.

One, forgetful of butterfat, to recall growing plump
with love and croissants in a Paris hotel.

One, compulsive as Sisyphus,
who tries to bake them at home.

Two to scrap over the last twisted-off end
as if fighting over a grant.

One, the perpetual child, to lick the plate clean,
brush crumbs from her bosom for birds.

And the one who first asked:
to lose count, be stuck with the check.

TABULA RASA

I dreamed a lover suggested
he should copy one of my poems
on my belly.

Not tattooed or embossed
but etched with a tiny knife
so sharp I'd feel no pain.

I wrote a quatrain
and he cut into me.
We are proud of our work.

But I'm always rewriting,
rewriting. And before dawn
he disappeared, whoever he was.

CHICAGO, 1938

When I became an angel
in the middle of Lake Shore Drive
all traffic stopped.

Lake Michigan, mere water before,
had frozen to a seeming shanty town
of igloos and huts,

blocks of platinum ice
jumbled on each other
by a careless architect.

Everything blizzarded over, I broke
free of my grandmother and two huge
Dalmatians stumbling in drifts.

Borne by wings of snow hooked together,
each crystal point tucked into lace
of tangent flakes, I took off

above that now unbounded thoroughfare,
left imprints of my flying feet
across the roofs of snowed-in cars,

then lay down to flail my arms,
describe half-circles in the snow,
mark the outline of myself.

No matter how often that road
has since been potholed, filled in,
jackhammered up, resurfaced yet again,

beneath asphalt and tar
still my tracery remains
white as an angel's wings.

THE MEMORY REQUIREMENT

for Mike Chen

What Mr. Chen, computer technician, means
by this term is as much an enigma as how
invisible letters jump from a skinny disk
to bounce around in that box like popcorn.

But here it must mean the demand of this mind
(from wilfulness or necessity)
to recall, rewrite, revoke, rearrange
its haphazard selections —

while time remains until the storm breaks,
lightning fractures the sky into fire, power
surges in spikes like brain waves on a drum,
my hard drive crashes, all memory is erased.

AFTERTHOUGHT

Like six computers pinging to one
another, Doctor, although the power's
off. Or high-tension lines singing
across plains in a blizzard.
I meant to tell you this morning.
Happens whenever I close my eyes.
A hive in the brain.

In a town, of course, there's always
an ambulance down the avenue,
fire engines across the park,
jackhammers, juke boxes, horns, brakes,
that school yard six blocks away,
trucks at the dump, a march,
hooves striking cobblestones.

Sounds pile up, are stored.
Volcanoes exploding decades ago
remain in the thickening air.
Cathedral chimes, warriors' drums,
troubadours' plaints, victims' moans,
those high-pitched notes
that set dogs howling.

That's what I hear, Doctor,
when I wake in the night
or nap after lunch.
A music box under my pillow,
roosters behind the drapes.
Has my skull become one vast
receptor? Do I also transmit?

I don't generate. I sit
in the armchair — no creaky
rocker for me — slippers padded,
phone unplugged. My necklaces
which used to tinkle and jangle —
I moved like a belled goat —
have been stolen. Or sold?

Still I hear their symphonies
on my bare neck. You might want
to send me for tests my next
check-up, next year. But today
I'm tuned to a fishmonger's serenade,
flocks of swans in the bay, and
from farther waters, choirs of whales.

SCOOPING THE MOON

> *"Illusion has been*
> *the downfall of many."*
> — *Tsuji Gettan, d. 1726*

Palms full of liquid light
the monkey scoops and scoops
the moon from the pond
to hang on his branch

steals moon slivers from water
till his fingers sprout flames
lips drink fire
always have light

Why should we gulp dust
glean mud from swamps
never dream of sunbeams
stars

VISITATIONS, PARK AVENUE

The camel hobbles over 79th and Park,
dugs dry as desert tombs.
Still, a string of twins,
some belonging to other beasts,
trails her over curbs.
She pants as if parched,
yet her stomach holds water enough
to cross the Equator.
Am I the only person to notice?
The camel nuzzles my hollows.
Buzz off, I tell her.
She clangs like a fire brigade,
gallops for blocks
into St. Pat's, where acolytes
tie velveteen curtains over her flanks.
She kicks them aside,
disappears through the sacristy,
non-stop out the rear doors.
The other animals also trot
somewhere into the night.
The acolytes return to their prayers.
I am still tracking spoor.

PROVOLONE

Cheese carries spores of its own destruction.
No metaphor this. True bluegreen spots,
impetigo in technicolor,
grow on my provolone.

But think: *microcosm,* or, go ahead, *metaphor.*
As on satellite maps, infrared,
where balding forests catch fire
and rivers run variants of crimson.

Even A-Bomb explosions: they burst
like volcanoes but programmed
to toadstool ivory/white
over the gleaming sea.

Except in reverse, a negative. That's how
mold spreads, and no matter
how virgin my plastic wrap
or aluminum foil

(bauxite and oil
dug up, pumped up
from the harassed Earth
scattering soil like spores,

on their way to becoming the shiny
prophylactics of kitchen life)
unable to shield
the cheese from itself.

Trace back to the cow. As if within
gullet and udder she bore
fungi, like diatoms in the ocean,
magnificent under a microscope.

So she, so we. All this
on my way to enrich
one bowl of anemic bouillon
with gratings of provolone.

I peel most of the mold
        into the trash to survive
        forever, prosper, infect
        even shards of glass.

Can't scrape it all. Although
        the surface looks creamy and clean,
        specks remain, spores
        will hide inside me

with those seeds of babies and wars,
        genius, disease, all
        awaiting their term,
        their turn to emerge.

AS THE OLD SPY PICKS UP A FIRST-CENTURY B.C.
PERFUME BOTTLE OF MOTTLED GLASS
SHEBA SWIMS INTO HIS SIGHT

And that night in Damascus
he rescued from six
Shiite vigilantes
the stately Ethiopian dancer
who claimed to descend
from King Solomon
via Emperor Menelik II
and carried within
the Ubangi-style rings
of her elongated lobes
a microfilmed Soviet plan
to occupy the African Horn.

Though Sheba was tall
he pretzeled her in
his Volkswagen trunk
and dressed like a trader
with crates of tomatoes
dried figs and dates
he gave the slip
to the Syrian militia
rabid Shiites, suave KGBniks.

They drove all night
to Palmyra where
under the desert moon
on a stone sarcophagus
inside a high
tower of tombs
Sheba insisted upon
expressing her three-
dimensional thanks
in cuneiform.

He mainlined antibiotics
for weeks, suffered
no ill effects
and gained one more
commendation for valor
under extreme duress.

As for Sheba
he got her into
a Master's Program
in Political Science
at Michigan State.

EATING CHEERIOS WHILE CONTEMPLATING
AN ALTERNATE LIFE FOR X
HAD SHE BEEN ALLOWED TO GROW UP IN FRANCE

for Colette Inez

Remember that playing Scrabble in French
would make different demands: a sudden
run on Xs, so few in the English set,

a shortage of Xs for crucifixes, crossroads,
X-chromosomes, star-crossed crosscurrents
crosspollinated, crossbred and cross-hatched,

and X-Marks-The-Spot that you
keep trying to find, catch in your
crossbow, crossfire, crosswise.

Consider the commonplace *aux.*
Everywhere *aux! aux! aux!*
pronounced like our O! O! O!

on some abandoned afternoon
under the crossvault
of an untended medieval abbey.

Or simply: X as in *aux noix,*
in this bilingual Cheerios box:
P'tits O dorés au miel et aux noix,

crunchy circles of oats
with honey and — Oh, nuts, as in:
a substitute for keener expletives

when, although one was brought up
not to be a crosspatch, "If you can't
say something nice, say nothing," still

you hoard X's to spell out cross words,
describe the strange crisscross of fate
across your checkered Scrabble board.

BOSSA NOVA

Laura, tressed with jasmine, wearing green
sheer as an aquarium, parades
along estrados through this delta town.

In damp cafes, men with onyx eyes
in chorus shift their mango hulks and sigh
when Laura arches past in four-four time.

Guaribas from the jungle howl her name
from dark within their furry simian throats.
Toucans swoop like multicolored ghosts.

In warm delirium of the steaming noon
she gradually unhems, unseams herself,
then in a dance of heat and dust

disintegrates into a hundred crumbs,
gives herself to every man, bird, beast,
until she is consumed, and they are full.

ICARUS, MANHATTAN

Across this fortressed isle
I move at a jerky pace
elbows at odds with my body

crawl step after step
one hundred flights up
slip between blades

of enormous fans silent
or spinning atop the shafts
of abandoned lifts

I hide for a while behind
cylinders of metallic water
net pigeons defeather

Purple loosestrife lures bees
I melt their wax
my skin catches fire

Dizzy I cling to the roof
at last kick off
flap dented wings falling

rise on currents of steam
and smoke over Hoboken
then soar over oceans

When updrafts peter out
I too will drop in the sea
but now I've learned to swim

146

FAMILY MATTERS

Sanson, French family of public executioners…Charles Henri
Sanson, 1740-93, guillotined Louis XVI. His son, Henri
Sanson, 1767-1840, was chief executioner in the Reign of
Terror: he guillotined Marie Antoinette.

Such tales Papa Charles must have told young Henri
at bedtime! How they inspired the child!
How proud he in turn would make his old dad

and later regale his own grandchildren, how hard
he toiled through the Reign, so much in demand, but oh,
what a plume in his hood to draw that particular dame

though her royal petticoats had fleas, and she was shorn.
The archives are poor in the family memoirs but
they must have passed anecdotes on at table

over *un bon potage*, lamb kidneys, calves' brains, blood
sausage, stuffed tripe, a crusty baguette to mop up,
and to finish off, a delicious *cœur à la crème*, Maman a whiz

in the kitchen. But what a time she surely had at market:
did neighbors peek in her basket, who knows what's beneath
those *artichauts*. Wiser to shop in another *quartier*.

And how did they choose a wife? She must scrub
splattered cloaks, mend hoods, darn gloves —
in the wash, *mon Dieu*, hand-me-downs take a beating.

Imagine the nuptial night, pillow talk in the dark,
then generations of babies bursting forth
headlong into their destined profession.

And if, *hélas*, it were a girl, how much dowry
was required, or could they marry her off
to some lad in the trade in a distant town?

And along with the wifely peck on both cheeks: *Au revoir,*
mon petit chou, don't forget your galoshes, bring home
a little memento for *Bébé*, and *chéri*, do have a nice day.

FROM THE COLLECTED WORKS

One page escaped the manuscript
on its way to the printers,
slipped between desk and wall,

stayed concealed like a hermit
who hides from unfriendly regimes
in Siberian wilds; or like

those pockets of Japanese troops
holed up in the jungle unaware that war
is over, only know they must wait

among banyans, ginger flowers and vines,
hoard the last grains of rice, live off
peculiar roots, keep bayonets sharp.

The poem hid in its niche years after
the rest were lauded or discarded...
Tonight it shows up, smudged and frayed,

as accustomed to silence as a recluse
snowed in for months in a shack,
who when company comes bursts forth

non-stop in dialect antique as that
seventeenth-century English preserved
in remote Appalachian valleys:

familiar yet antiquated, odd.
Still, one welcomes the prodigal
back to the fold.

ON OPENING A BRAND-NEW HALF-STITCHED
BOOK OF POETRY

But the binding inside
page fifteen frays —
heavy ivory strings,
plumb lines to an image, idea,
are guy wires to lace
across the face of the poem,
weave a web —

Each thread catches the hook
of a letter,
s, c, g or *z,*
even ties onto an *o,*
and, like childhood's loose teeth
which hung on too long
(teeth, childhood, all),
yank meanings from words,
the bite from the line —

Quickly, read quickly, in case
the page disappears from the poem —

VIII.
THRIFT AND GOODWILL

STONED FRUIT

I choose
the bruised
ripe bargains but

if I find just
rockhard plums,
peaches, pears

I bring them home
like beach stones
for the sill

or cradle them
between my breasts
perhaps they'll hatch

or leave them in
the chipped brown bowl
shaped by a friend

whose husband shot
her lover though
I now think it was he

who made the bowl
for me, the fruit
ripens so fast

PLACE SETTINGS

My mother's plates, gold-rimmed
Limoges, all matched, could serve
soup, fish, roast, salad, fruit,
cake and demi-tasses for thirty guests.

In my house, every dish is different.
Not just because six kids will break
six plates apiece within six years,
but husbands do get shaky, mad, or drunk.

Better they throw plates than us,
and I haunt yard sales and Goodwill,
glean jetsam from strange women's lives
perhaps as hazardous as mine but tidier:

when their wedding china dwindles
with the husbands, children, years,
to seven saucers, one chipped cup,
they dump them at the church bazaar.

I hoard poor-cousin cups, orphaned plates,
enrich my stock with fresh gene pools
from other clans, so what if one bowl's plum
clashes with the platter's rose.

I conjure how another's nicks,
chips and cracks occurred,
weigh her losses and my own
bargains and diversities.

SILVER

Mostly stainless steel gussied up
like real silver, they glitter through
their nicks, flecks of rust, bent prongs.

What doesn't shine may even be sterling.
Grayed, tinged blueblack, camouflaged
as if ashamed of how it's fallen.

Yet an old duchess hit by hard times
might just polish up…Discreetly, I spit
on the bowl of one dingy spoon, rub until

my finger turns black, the spot emits a shy gleam.
Illegible symbols on the back of the shaft
hint lineage, simplicity intimates taste.

Each piece in the bin costs 25 cents.
At home, it takes hours
to find polish, pry up childproof caps,

scour first with brass polish, then gunk
for silver. Fingers aching, I buff
the whole spoon to a dull, very dull, glow.

Most silver's gone. How many washings, how many mouths,
and whose…New: a shimmering gift to a long-ago bride.
Worn thin: hand-me-down to a fourth daughter's dowry.

Too drab to join my Grandmama's matched set adorned
with curlicues, monograms, every piece radiant, unscratched.
Yet I can't relegate this — prize — to the kitchen.

So it stays in my cluttered study where I allow
only poets, exiles and refugees, my tarnished familiars,
friends with unfortunate histories, a story to tell.

ON THE EVE OF A SALVATION ARMY PICKUP

Like this old tee-
shirt you've kept
since school

where the stains
now form part
of the fabric.

You could not
discard this
or rag it:

Did you lose your
virginity in it
or win a team cup,

later wear it
to paint a house,
a portrait, the town...

FOUR POTATOES

"They'll poison you, green," Aunt Tanya warns.
"Such a waste! Potatoes are all one needs
for a meal, topped with sour cream, dill."

I bought them beige, if pocked and scarred,
from the REDUCED FOR QUICK SALE cart,
did not shade them from treacherous light.

But I grew up with tales of potato famines,
the knowledge that wealth and life can disappear
with a drought, revolution or war, so hoard

those holey clothes, expired tinned fish, rutabagas.
Four dangerous spuds, like stones in a stream green
round their gills, loll weeks on my shelf.

Suddenly now the bottom ends (which side is the top?)
sprout rosy goose barnacles: tiny green fingers probe air
the way tentacles fathom the sea. A miracle born of neglect.

Might these nascent roots? tendrils? leaves? transmute
into creatures to stalk the yard, or feed the neighborhood...
I seize the cleaver, chop, plant sixteen cubes in my window box.

ONIONS

One slice: pain
needles my eyes.
But you want onions.

Through tears
translucent as onion
skin, I cut again.

Undaunted by old wives'
defenses — cold water,
needle-in-my-teeth,

this knife — vapors
invade and occupy
old wounds.

At last, as when confronting
you, I choose to lose
whatever argument,

throw these alabaster globes
whole into the pot:
in heat they'll slip apart

like Chinese puzzle boxes,
resolve themselves...
Will we? They too stay

vengeful, won't be tamed.
I serve you onions
blind as love.

HAND-TO-MOUTH

Yes, that's how I live
in the literal sense
now you're away.

I hang out in twenty-four-hour
diners, the kind
with pie à la mode,
two refills of coffee free,
the radio always on.

I space out my visits
and always pay for my tea.
When the owner is out
the waitress brings soup.
Crackers and water come with.
And they have vinyl banquettes.

This morning the waitress
insisted I try a bite
from her steaming pan
of fresh-baked liver
sprinkled with sesame seeds.

I'm still vegetarian, darling,
but never, oh never, have I
tasted anything quite so good
as that liver with sesame seeds...
I almost asked for the recipe.

But who knows how long
I'll be out sampling
the tiny seven-grain cubes
on the Bakery counter,
hotdog slivers in barbecue sauce
the supermarket's promoting,
the new labels of punch
doled into thimble-sized cups...

I market-test everything.
I buy just enough packets of chips
or from the Bargain Cart
spotted apples and rotten pears —

"Fruit tastes better ripe," I tell
the well-coiffed cashier who watches
I don't run off with the escarole,
yellow peppers, ruby radicchio.

I skip the marked-down potatoes:
nowadays I don't cook.
Hairy carrots, squidgy zucchini,
I scrape with your Swiss army knife
and scrub with snow in the park.

Squirrels leap through the drifts
to eat from my table.
Some days the sun's out,
dances on patches of ice.

I must watch my step
on the unshoveled walks,
but how you and I would skate
on the frozen pool. They've shut
off the fountain for winter.

Some days I go to the library
or take a subway — how many
invisible miles, peculiar people...

In the bus station one night
I found myself curled around
by a girl in her twenties
also come in from the snow,
each of us wrapped
in our separate coats
cloaking each other.

Sometimes I pass her now
on the avenue. We don't speak,
though our eyes for an instant meet.

Her fortune seems to have changed,
or she's dressed for a better role:
spike-heeled boots, and a fur.

Even at 20 below I still wear
my tweed coat, prudent galoshes,
the red dress you bought me,
my velvet hat with the veil.

Once a week I go home to check
if there's mail left outside,
but never go in. The day you
departed, I stopped the papers.

But I keep up with the news —
classifieds left on a bench,
stock market reports from a bin —
Yes, you're doing all right —
I read whatever cover-to-cover.

What luck, today's horoscope!
My stars predict dining out,
a new romance in the offing
or else an old one resumes.

I await more precise information,
and perhaps a postcard.

AS AFTER A THIRTY-YEARS' WAR: OLD LOVERS

They remember every word we spoke, our
smoked oysters, rum balls, coffee *mit schlag*, served
with sweet promises of love eternal
when they moved on. For like rivers they are

always in flux, though some dry up. We plod
dusty wadis through deserts, but glance back
over our shoulders should the current lack
of lovers turn into a sudden flood.

Yes! Old codgers trickle in, then waves flow
toward our doors. Yet bloated, or bony, shrunk...
White-bristled billy goats. Bunioned hooves clunk
over our thresholds. Still hungry, they know

we are a soft touch. They were our soul mates
once. Now, we confront our doubles, our fate.

IX.
IN THIS WINGED INSTANT

HURRICANE, CAPE HATTERAS

Like diving into late September surf
midpoint between red flags,

I've plunged into love again and again.
This time I've never known the waves

to be so high. And strong:
somersaulted me over and over,

double immelmanns, loop-the-loops, undertow
so fierce it would not give me back —

> In Rio once a huge wave picked me up,
> toppled me from the crest, dropped me
>
> on bare sand uncushioned
> by any ragged wake of spume,
>
> knocked me senseless as the next
> wave engulfed, pulled me out —

This time, the risk
might be worth the trip.

Beach empty, endless,
gusts tumbling pelicans,

dolphins slicing platinum waves,
walls of sea beige from swirling

tons of sand — Such weight, such force!
If by chance, dumb luck, I drown,

it will be at the apogee of bliss,
more would be superfluous —

NORTH OF THE AIRBASE, AT HOME

We finish breakfast but stay in bed
reading the papers, grow sleepy.
You reach to encircle me.
                              Suddenly
thunder bombards over the soy bean fields —
windows rattle, the whole house shakes,
plates fall from shelves —

Explosions downriver.
That triangular zone on Bay charts
where red print warns:
                              TARGET PRACTICE.

Silence.

The house resettles on its old stones.
Crickets retune their legs.
The sun kindles the sheets.

We make love
though my mind flutters off
to pilots adjusting their dials,
aiming for perfect hits.

Now you're asleep.
I dress, boil fresh tea.

Inside the sun porch
a butterfly beats the panes:
mourning cloak, black wings
marked with false eyes red-orange
as rifle fire in the night.

I capture him in cupped hands,
release him over the Queen Anne's lace.

He catches an updraft,
                              soars off.

Dust remains dark on my palms.

RESIDENTS

Our walls house squirrels,
raccoons, mice, whatever else
no cat can reach, or dares.

Don't they mind our noise —
Beethoven, Bach, clatter
of dishes, tea kettle whistle,

hum and roar of machines?
Heavy Metal might drive them out
along with the neighborhood.

Have they become our familiars
who know what bounty we offer
of melon seeds, fish bones and crusts

in the trash can whose lid
is too dented to shut...
Or they hang in as reminders:

we're none of us safe. Only they
seem secure and eternal between
layers of dry wall and brick

with their more predictable patterns
of tumbles and squabbles and hungers
and times to curl into furry

circles of love and sleep,
and their skill at gnawing anew
secret entrances under the eaves.

IN THIS WINGED INSTANT —

1. July

Dragonflies hover over the dock,
swallows dart from nests underneath,

gulls settle into a semicircle
across the harbor mouth,

a spangled fritillary
perches on my palm,

a cormorant lands on a piling against
the red sun dappling a graying bay,

and already the first bats
scythe the wake of the rising moon,

there are indeed only yourself and myself
in an instant that will also take flight.

2. December

Fox prints and deer pock the snow
over the grass where we danced.

Our picnic table hosts banquets of snow.
Canvas chairs tip snow onto snow.

Skeletal weeds poke through crust.
The fig bush bears a snow harvest.

Beyond the shiver of beach, crabs
have shuffled deep in the channel,

fish fled under ice, or south. I don't
adjust to this change of season, still

long for summer, as for you, utterly.
Then a hundred swans avalanche to the cove.

BEYOND THE ASPARAGUS FIELD

Last August I crawled between feathery stalks
hunting unseasonal shoots for a final feast.

Now, snow fills the furrows, mounded rows hide
frozen tubers, vermilion pods, thistle seeds.

Mole tunnels ripple the snow,
buckle under my boots. Flash of dark fur —

Gooseprints pattern the field. Beyond
lies a pond encircled by willows,

milkweed, cattails, goldenrod,
purple loosestrife turned brown.

One foot on the edge, I kick snow aside.
The ice is wrinkled but firm.

I race home, shout for skates and for you,
grab the shovel, recross the field,

scrape a diagonal path, clear
one quadrant, perimeter next,

a track for speedskaters like us.
You stride over reeds, note cracks in my ice.

"No skates anywhere, and it's getting dark."
"Come on, we can slide anyhow — "

You're doubtful but, mittens to gloves,
we polonaise to invisible fiddles, circle

and glide in our usual dangerous dance
until the dizzy moon harrows the pond,

asparagus spears puncture the snow,
wind feathers more snow over ice.

IN YOUR ABSENCE

As when on the iced rind of January's pond,
among cattails already shedding
their dust of seed —

more numberless than sperm, they would fertilize
Earth, so why isn't our whole globe
one wall-to-wall cattail battalion —

As now, on the pond, I think: summer,
the murk live, the surface licking clouds,
luring mosquitoes and frogs.

Glazed distance and thick ice
wall off the sun from deadened frogs
and you from me.

Give me a clear pane and, in winter's settled time,
I would see bottom, the muck a treasury
of squiggly things churning

inside themselves, in silence, waiting —
Cycles of love begun in mud but sparked
in waves glowing, water on fire —

In another season, pondweed dense, I fell for you
quick as a frog who springs from green
cattails into its own ripples,

and will again when the pond's
impenetrable rind dissolves
beneath a closer sun.

MAY DAY MOON

I would swim with you in the moon
full tonight, splitting the sea
so close we could reach it in a few strokes.

Quickly! Let's spur our horses out there
before the moon climbs the stairway of clouds —

We'll stand on the horses' backs,
snatch the moon's golden ring,
perch like dragonflies on its white rind —

then drop into that milky vat
to drown, or find pearls —

STRANGER MOONS

*"Strange moons swim into conjunction at times
of transition."*

— *Charles Trueheart*

I too am swimming, caught
in the net of stars caught
on water wavering, we waver
into each other's orbits.

Orion turns upside down,
Mars is a medusa
reddish and gravid,
Venus, sunstable, wet,

while the moon recreates itself
over and over, the wake broken
discs of unreliable light
ephemeral as pebbles

skipping across water, wafers
of moon, discs of stone,
transiting from earth and air
to water flecked with tiny fires.

Whether at any time
moons swim with the rays,
bounce with blowfish on sand,
melt with medusas on sunny beaches,

nothing is ever still,
nothing exactly moves,
everything changes in time
or nothing at all.

SORTING LAUNDRY

Folding clothes,
I think of folding you
into my life.

Our king-sized sheets
like table cloths
for the banquets of giants,

pillow cases, despite so many
washings seams still
holding our dreams.

Towels patterned orange and green,
flowered pink and lavender,
gaudy, bought on sale,

reserved, we said, for the beach,
refusing, even after years,
to bleach into respectability.

So many shirts and skirts and pants
recycling week after week, head over heels
recapitulating themselves.

All those wrinkles
to be smoothed, or else
ignored, they're in style.

Myriad uncoupled socks
which went paired into the foam
like those creatures in the ark.

And what's shrunk
is tough to discard
even for Goodwill.

In pockets, surprises:
forgotten matches,
lost screws clinking on enamel,

paper clips, whatever they held
between shiny jaws, now
dissolved or clogging the drain,

well-washed dollars, legal tender
for all debts public and private,
intact despite agitation,

and, gleaming in the maelstrom,
one bright dime,
broken necklace of good gold

you brought from Kuwait,
the strangely tailored shirt
left by a former lover...

If you were to leave me,
if I were to fold
only my own clothes,

the convexes and concaves
of my blouses, panties, stockings, bras
turned upon themselves,

a mountain of unsorted wash
could not fill
the empty side of the bed.

on the marge of Lake Laberge

Elisavietta Ritchie's fiction, poetry, creative non-fiction, and translations from Russian and French have appeared in *Poetry, The American Scholar, New York Times, The Christian Science Monitor, Washington Post, National Geographic, New York Quarterly, Press, Confrontation, New Letters, Kalliope, Nimrod, Canadian Women's Studies, Calyx, Iris*; a variety of anthologies including *When I'm An Old Woman I Shall Wear Purple; If I Had My Life To Live Over I Would Pick More Daisies; The Tie That Binds; If I Had A Hammer: Women's Work; Grow Old Along With Me/The Best Is Yet To Be; Generation to Generation; Gifts of the Fathers; Diamonds Are A Girl's Best Friend*, and numerous other publications.

Flying Time: Stories & Half-Stories includes four PEN Syndicated Fiction winners. Among her books of poetry are *Elegy For The Other Woman: new and selected terribly female poems; Tightening The Circle Over Eel Country,* which won the Great Lakes Colleges Association's New Writer's Prize for Best First Book of Poetry; *Raking The Snow,* which won the Washington Writer's Publishing House 1981-82 competition; and the chapbooks *A Wound-Up Cat and Other Bedtime Stories, A Sheaf of Dreams And Other Games, Moving To Larger Quarters, The Problem With Eden,* and two novellas in verse, *Timbot* and *Wild Garlic: The Journal of Maria X.* Her work has been translated into more than a dozen languages.

She has read at the Library of Congress, Harbourfront, Folger Library, Pittsburgh International Forum, and many other cultural centers, libraries, universities and schools in the United States, Canada, Brazil, around the Far East, Australia, New Zealand, Russia, and the Balkans. She often teaches creative writing workshops and serves as a poet-in-the-schools.

She founded The Wineberry Press, and for three years was president of Washington Writers' Publishing House, a collaborative press. She edited *The Dolphin's Arc: Poems on Endangered Creatures of the Sea* and other books, and occasionally photographs for *The New York Times* and elsewhere.

Although home base is Washington DC and the Patuxent River in Southern Maryland, she has traveled widely and lived in Malaysia, Cyprus, Lebanon, France, Canada, and most recently in Australia. She is married to Clyde Farnsworth, a *New York Times* correspondent and novelist. She has three children and two stepsons.

On *Flying Time: Stories and Half-Stories*, which includes four PEN Syndicated Fiction winners:

"Now and then one wishes for prose that can be taken in small but satisfying measure, like Chopin or ice cream...*Flying Time* by Elisavietta Ritchie, Signal Books, is the first full-length collection of prose from a poet who richly commends words and memories, infusing these stories with vivid, tight, penetrating language. She remembers walks with her father, waterside snippets, a lifetime of treasures, with a final walk beside his wheelchair toward a picnic of eels. Ritchie shares teatime in Leningrad, dreams and nightmares of War years on the farm, arguments over the costs of a coffin, impressions of priests in a Russian church far from home in Chicago. And delicious, mysterious descriptions of bugs, flowers, birds, brick walls, and efforts to scare away rats with a cap pistol discovered in a neglected attic. She even captures the occasional, strange allure of sorting laundry: 'Our king-sized sheets like tablecloths for the banquets of giants, pillowcases, despite so many washings, still hold our dreams.' More than 50 stories here, a constellation of bright, illuminating tales."

The Book Reader

"I read *Flying Time* with enormous enjoyment. It reveals delicate witchery and a teeming imagination...I was crossing horizons of the spirit."

D.M. Thomas, author of *The White Hotel*

"Glows with the right word in the absolutely right place, unerringly chosen to set the mood and tone. Hints of Dostoyevsky and the families of Tolstoy in the works of a woman of today! Provocative!"

Mary Sue Koeppel, *Kalliope: A Journal of Women's Art*

DATE DUE